the
softer side
of
leadership

"A big title or position will only get you so far. Leaders who truly influence are the ones who rise to the top through these softer skills of leadership. Gene Habecker does a masterful job of explaining these intangibles of leadership that are essential. These skills are the reason that he has been so beloved throughout his career and why he has been able to lead at such high levels. This book is extremely insightful, and these skills are non-negotiable for anyone who wants to reach their full leadership potential."

Heather Larson, Executive Pastor/Incoming Lead Pastor, Willow Creek Community Church, South Barrington, Illinois

"I needed this book. I needed the vivid reminders, the fresh insights and the compelling perspectives. Frankly, I don't ever remember reading a book on leadership that I didn't want to put down. Until this one. One chapter after another provided conviction, grace, and hope. They were a magnet to my heart, water to a thirsty soul. Gene Habecker has been a leader I've respected for many years. His insights are tested and true. Honesty, humility, and wisdom mark each page. Prepare to be inspired."

Dan Wolgemuth, President/CEO, Youth for Christ

"There are many good business books that answer the question: How is great leadership experienced? Topics might range from how to build a great team, to the importance of clear strategic direction, to operational excellence, to a myriad of like topics. *The Softer Side of Leadership* addresses a different issue: How is mature leadership developed? The book is a robust exploration of the deep interior work necessary to be a leader of substance. The ongoing disciplines that yield secure, wise, and centered leadership are counterintuitive. But they feel right and they bring good. We need this brand of leadership. We need this book."

Thomas Addington, PhD, Head of Company, Givington's

"This book will go with me when I travel and stay on my desk when I am at home. It will be a resource to me and one to share with others working to combine the *soft* and *hard* skills required for effective leadership. In my 45 years in academic medicine, I have worked with many bright people and almost none of them have failed because they lacked the *hard* skills. Almost all leadership failures I have observed, and there have been many over the years, have resulted from the lack of the *soft* skills Gene unpacks. While others have sprinkled biblical quotes throughout their work to achieve some measure of spiritual credibility, Gene not only has integrated Biblical truth with leadership wisdom, he has demonstrated that biblical truth is the basis for such wisdom. This is not a casual read. It will require reflection, and this will require time, or as Gene writes, some *sacred space*. A commitment to finding such space is important and reading this book will make this worth the effort."

**R. Dale Lefever, PhD, Organizational Consultant and
Emeritus Faculty, University of Michigan Medical School**

"Peter Drucker invented management science by making a simple but profound case: managers are needed to make knowledge effective. My friend Gene Habecker makes a similar case for human flourishing. In order for organizations, and indeed societies, to thrive, leaders must develop the soft skills of employees to ensure highest and best use of hard skills. This book will show you how."

**Jay Hein, President, Sagamore Institute, and former director,
the White House Office of Faith-based and Community Initiatives**

"The author demonstrates true soft skills of leadership in his life. We saw this as his colleagues on the Global Board of the United Bible Societies (UBS) and some of us, also under his leadership as the President of the UBS Executive Board. We all could not believe how humble he was, and yet, at the same time, he was President of the American Bible Society. He made us feel important and appreciated. To me, this is the summary of true soft skills, so ably explained in this book. This book is enjoyable to read and provides helpful, practical lived-life experiences. I could not put down this book once I started reading it. Many will gain from reading it."

Ambassador Dr. Mary M. Khimulu, MBS; Former Kenya Ambassador/ Permanent Delegate of Kenya to UNESCO, Paris

"I am grateful to Gene Habecker for writing a book like this. I found that it pulled me in. I had simply wanted to read it from cover to cover but couldn't do that. It touched me deeply and I needed to meditate on each chapter. I began to use it during my morning devotional time, which I never do with any book. I found that what was written was deeply spiritual and after reading each chapter, I needed to evaluate myself and my actions and take note of changes needed. Absorb chaos, emit peace, give hope, forgive, be a great follower to lead, Sabbath rest, listen, and love. This book was a great check-up and an encouragement for me to do better. I have a small group of books, among the many I read, that I buy to share with others. This one will be among them."

Morgan Jackson, Director, Faith Comes by Hearing

"Dr. Gene Habecker's book appeals to leaders who are dissatisfied with the canned MBA approach to leadership. He persuasively discusses the seemingly less important aspects of leadership, those soft skills that underlie and reveal a leader's character and sustain his or her organizational effectiveness. Drawing on a lifetime of experiences, including candid revelation of his own mistakes, Habecker illustrates the power of quality interactions with people. In serving with him on a board of trustees, I have observed Dr. Habecker lead a university through a series of crises with exceptional competence. At critical junctures, his embodiment of 'qualitative skills, practices, habits, disciplines, and attitudes that characterize how people interact and behave with one another' was subjected to public scrutiny, and distinguished by remarkable approval. Drawing not only on wisdom forged through his successes and failures, Dr. Habecker generously includes insights from delightfully variegated sources. I enthusiastically recommend *The Softer Side of Leadership* for those who are ready and willing to lead from the inside out."

Paige Comstock Cunningham, JD, PhD, Executive Director, The Center for Bioethics & Human Dignity, Trinity International University

"This is not a theoretical book; most importantly, it is a greatly needed practical and personal one based on real and meaningful experience. As Gene rightly points out, this is a book not *about* leadership but *as* leadership. Gene shares some unique and powerful insights drawn from his extensive and successful leadership of two universities and an international faith-based organization, places where he has served together with his very special wife and partner Marylou. For leaders, and those aspiring to be leaders, this is indeed excellent and essential reading."

Roberto Laver, SJD, Founder/Director, FIDES, former World Bank Senior Counsel, and Harvard Law School Visiting Fellow

"*The Softer Side of Leadership* is a wonderful book that focuses on the part of leadership that is often not included in degree programs or textbooks, but is quintessential to being successful. This important resource for leaders is filled with practical, personal examples that makes it hard to put down. He captures your attention by sharing the wisdom he has gained by leading organizations and colleges over the past 35 years. The softer skills addressed in this book—behaviors, attitudes, and practices—are often overlooked. People with great business skills often fail, because they don't understand the power of the kinds of things addressed in this book, such as creativity, maintaining a sacred space, or staying connected to the heart. This book may hold the key as to why some leaders fail. While there are religious examples in the book, it has invaluable information for anyone who reads it regardless of their religious background. This book is good for potential leaders as well as for those who want to be more successful in their leadership positions."

**Dr. Rhonda Jeter, PhD, Professor, and Dean,
College of Education, Bowie State University**

"A must-read for all active and aspiring leaders in business and non-profit sectors, as well as in churches and mission agencies. This is a practical and creative exposition of soft skills, seen as indispensable competencies for effective leadership. Here is an invaluable resource for all leaders, particularly for those longing to be 'the salt of the earth' in 'winner take all' environments."

**Fergus Macdonald, PhD, Honorary Chairperson, Lausanne
Committee, and retired General Secretary, United Bible Societies**

"My friend, Dr. Eugene Habecker, captures the heartbeat of Christ-like leadership. In *The Softer Side of Leadership*, Gene teaches leaders how to effectively care for themselves and the people they serve every day. The best part is that he practices what he preaches. Whether you're a CEO, pastor, or parent, I urge you to come sit at the feet of this wise, seasoned shepherd. Not only will you become a more effective leader, you'll become a happier, holier person as well."

Roy Peterson, President & CEO, American Bible Society

the
softer side
of
leadership

Essential Soft Skills That Transform
Leaders and the People They Lead

EUGENE B.
HABECKER

The Softer Side of Leadership: Essential Soft Skills That Transform Leaders and the People They Lead
© 2018 Eugene B. Habecker
Published by Deep River Books
Sisters, Oregon
www.deepriverbooks.com

Unless otherwise noted, all Scripture notations are taken from the Holy Bible, New Living Translation, copyright © 1996, 2004, 2007, 2013, 2015 by Tyndale House Foundation. Used by permission of Tyndale House Publishers, Inc., Carol Stream, Illinois 60188. All rights reserved.

Scripture notations marked (CEV) are taken from the Contemporary English Version®. Copyright © 1995 American Bible Society. All rights reserved.

Scripture notations marked (KJV) are taken from the King James Version. Public domain.

Scripture notations marked (MSG) are taken from *The Message*. Copyright © 1993, 1994, 1995, 1996, 2000, 2001, 2002. Used by permission of NavPress Publishing Group.

Scripture notations marked (HCSB) are taken from the Holman Christian Standard Bible. Copyright © 1999, 2000, 2002, 2003, 2009 by Holman Bible Publishers, Nashville Tennessee. All rights reserved.

Scripture notations marked (GNT) taken from the Good News Translation in Today's English Version, Second Edition. Copyright © 1992 by American Bible Society. Used by Permission.

ISBN—13: 9781632694683

Library of Congress: 2018933194

Printed in the USA
2018—First Edition

Cover design by Connie Gabbert

Table of Contents

Dedication and Acknowledgments

Dedication

I begin by dedicating this book to my incredible and loving wife, Marylou, who has walked with me in marriage for almost five decades and who has served with me in many leadership roles. We have had the joy of "professing the presidency together" at three special places. Marylou has been my best leadership teacher and primary accountability partner. More importantly, she has been the person who has taught me the most about soft skills and about leading and following, and has done so with simple grace and elegance.

I also dedicate this book to each of our children and their loving and supportive families. They have asked me penetrating questions. They have challenged my ideas. They have taught and continue to teach me about leading and following. They model the values discussed in this book within their own families and among those they lead and serve.

Acknowledgments

The acknowledgement list is long, but out of necessity I need to keep it brief. It begins with Dr. Dennis Hensley, professor of professional writing at Taylor University. He has been a consistent critic, encourager, and counselor throughout this writing process, and his contributions are many and invaluable. Kelli Taylor, who faithfully served as my executive assistant in the Taylor presidency, was a tremendous support in the early versions of manuscript drafts. Anna Oelerich has diligently helped in the later stages of manuscript preparation.

The professional support staff at Deep River Books has been exceptional. I am so grateful to long-term friends Bill and Nancie Carmichael who have encouraged in inestimable ways. The strong support of Carl Simmons as a gifted editor has added so much to making this project better. Altogether, the Deep River Books staff has provided untiring professional guidance throughout this publishing process.

Finally, I want to acknowledge the influence of hundreds of people in various roles and contexts with whom I have interacted over multiple decades, as we discussed leadership topics in both employment and volunteer situations. This would include thousands of students, faculty, staff, and the boards where we were able to serve in the university world, as well as the hundreds of colleagues in both the US and overseas where we were able to engage in leadership discussions as part of our varied involvements with the American Bible Society. These gifted people have taught me much about leading and following—something I'm still at work learning.

All praise to God, for however He allows this book to be used, for His purposes and for His glory.

Introduction

"Little value has traditionally been given to . . . so-called soft skills."
—Michael Grothaus[1]

"A total of 58% [of hiring managers across the US] said the lack of soft skills among job seekers was 'limiting their company's productivity.'"
—Emilie Rusch, *The Denver Post*, September 4, 2016

"It was a big mess. I had trouble during the interview. I totally missed what they were looking for in their job applicants. Unfortunately, I didn't get the job—didn't even come close."

William was one of those "can't miss" job candidates. With both undergraduate and graduate degrees from "top five" US universities, and armed with solid entry-level and mid-level leadership experience in appropriate organizations, he thought he was prepared to make the transition to senior leadership. He got the appointment for the "finalist" interview but ultimately wasn't hired.

So, what happened? He got the "financials" and the "metrics" right and said all the right things in his reports. He understood the financials, his draft business plan was well done, and he was outstanding in his use of analytics. But people seemed distant from his presentations and seemed underwhelmed when he cast his vision for the future. William was confused about the reaction to his interview.

He had the right information, had presented the right facts, had studied the appropriate academic subjects, and thought he had the right workplace experiences. He had mastered the right quantitative skill sets in his respective degree programs. Where had he gone wrong? What issues had he missed?

What William had failed to understand is that leaders need to possess and exercise a variety of soft skills—behaviors, practices, and attitudes that contribute to leadership effectiveness: "While the hard skills are essential to getting the interview, it's the soft skills that will land the job."[2] Daniel Goleman notes, "Of course high performance in academics and the right technical skills still matter. But in today's job market the best employers are looking for something in addition . . . companies 'want graduates with soft skills.'"[3] An article in the *Harvard Business Review* adds, "Most leaders . . . tend to emphasize their strength, competence, and credentials in the workplace, but that is exactly the wrong approach. Leaders who project strength before establishing trust (a soft skill) run the risk of eliciting fear."[4]

Many who aspire to be organizational leaders limit their leadership development to acquiring more knowledge and information—more "competence training" learning, and more "hard" skills and information about what leaders do. Developing competencies in "hard skills" is an important part of understanding leadership. But effective leadership requires more than just hard skill acquisition. It also requires soft skills and behaviors about work and the workplace. How are soft skills and hard skills different?

Soft Skills v. Hard Skills

There are multiple common sources that provide basic distinctions. Soft skills, for instance, are sometimes described as "personal attributes that enhance an individual's interactions, job performance and career prospects. Unlike hard skills, which tend to be specific to a certain type of task or activity, soft skills are broadly applicable."[5]

Another source observes that "Soft skills are a cluster of person-ality traits that characterize one's relationships in a milieu. These skills . . . include social graces, communication abilities, language skills, personal habits, cognitive or emotional empathy, time man-agement, teamwork, and leadership traits."[6] Soft skills tend to lean in the direction of qualitative expectations more so than quantita-tive ones. Soft skills drive us to look inside, at the parts of us that cannot be easily identified or measured. Alternately, "Hard skills . . . are about a person's skill set and ability to perform a certain type of task or activity."[7]

As used in this book, soft skills represent a collection of primar-ily qualitative skills, behaviors, practices, habits, disciplines, and attitudes that characterize how people interact and behave with one another. Whereas only a few will be addressed in this effort, in my leadership experience I have found all of them to be necessary and essential to leadership effectiveness.

As an illustration, I often explain to students that effective lead-ers have to do multiple things well, but that in crisis situations, three things must be done *exceptionally* well: absorb chaos, give calm, and provide hope. These are all qualitative behaviors, not quantita-tive ones. Crises come at leaders from all directions; they include natural disasters and personal tragedies that deeply affect organi-zations and their people. During those times, leaders must actively engage each of these three behaviors, all at the same time. Effective leaders develop them as soft skills.

Two days from my inauguration as president of Taylor University, we experienced one of those kinds of crises, as we lost four outstand-ing students and a staff member in a tragic tractor-trailer accident less than five miles from campus. The campus was reduced to great sorrow. I remember being in a packed auditorium as we all expec-tantly waited for news and, ultimately, the names of those who lost their lives. I had no choice but to attempt to absorb the chaos of those moments while providing some semblance of calm for our grieving campus community. At the same time I had to provide hope—hope that somehow God would give all of us strength to get through this, especially the parents and families who had experienced loss. Absorbing the chaos, giving back calm, and providing hope goes way beyond rational competency and skills. People were looking to me to find out if I really cared for those students and staff lost in the accident. They were less interested in my trying to rationalize pain and suffering, and more interested in my helping all of us together to grieve our campus loss. To do so required that I display my softer side, reflecting soft skills in everything I did or said.

To be sure, there are not always clear lines of demarcation between hard and soft skills. On the one hand, "hard skills" seem to focus more on what leaders do, whereas "soft skills" tend to focus on how leaders lead. Those championing "soft skills" also tend to include an intentional focus on the importance of attitudes and behaviors that reflect commitment, character, integrity, teamwork, emotional health, and self-management in their relationships.

A report from a *McKinsey Quarterly* interview with Chinese business leaders illustrates this new learning and understanding about the difference between hard and soft skills: "The 'softer skills' are a leadership necessity for all leaders in China: things like teamwork, communications, presentations, culture—all the skills that help you deal with people. Leadership is built on these skills, but in the past, Tsinghua was only strong in the 'hard' analytical skills: things like accounting, mathematics, science, and engineering." Another Chinese business leader noted, "Successful executives develop their intuition."[8]

Many books and articles focus on these hard skills, essentially the stuff of what leaders do—quantitative and analytical skills, including process development, change management, project management, strategic planning, strategy development and deployment, and marketing. Words such as measurement, assessment, sustainability, and policy and procedures manuals are all part of the "hard skills" vocabulary. It is not that hard skills are irrelevant or unnecessary. They are quite relevant and necessary to mission accomplishment and fulfillment. The point is simply that their mastery is not enough to achieve mission effectiveness. Soft skills are also needed.

Only since the mid-1990s has soft-skill leadership literature begun to emerge in more visible ways. It's not that soft-skill acquisition is new; rather, the link between the acquisition of soft skills and the impact of effective organizational leadership is now better understood.

Soft skills can be learned and developed. A simple awareness of their need and importance is a place to begin. The soft skills discussed in this book—and only a relative handful are referenced—are skills and behaviors often overlooked or underemphasized in organizational leadership. Given their vital role for effective leadership, they are simply too important to be ignored. That's what this book is all about—the increasing importance of soft skills as necessary and essential parts of leadership.

It is imperative to note from the beginning that leadership and leaders are distinctive and serve in unique contexts. Whereas leaders exercise similar functions and carry out common tasks in terms of what they do, how that is done depends totally on the individual leader and the leadership context. A brief review puts that in perspective.

Leadership in Perspective—a Brief Overview

For thousands of years we humans have struggled with this idea of leadership, trying to wrap our arms around a better understanding of just what it means to be a leader. From the earliest stories of the Jewish leaders in the Bible, the teachings of Jesus of Nazareth—who, by the way, cautioned his followers to avoid the term "leader"[9]—to the contemporary sage on the stage, there have been (and most likely will continue to be) efforts to better understand leadership. The hope is that we leaders will eventually find some ultimate leadership elixir, embedded with all of the appropriate leadership strategies and tactical steps and habits, to ensure organizational success. Isn't that what we want?

Barbara Kellerman, writing in the *Harvard Business Review*,[10] is representative of those who have studied leaders throughout time. She has studied the work of many leaders and others who have offered perspectives on leadership. David McCullough's efforts, particularly his popular *John Adams* and his Pulitzer Prize-winning *Truman*, are additional examples of leadership narratives, as are the writings of Eric Metaxas about William Wilberforce and Dietrich Bonhoeffer. Each of the subjects of these efforts has something to teach us about leadership.

Writing in *Forbes*, Rich Karlgaard notes what probably most in leadership have discovered: "Leadership . . . is not a formula. You can't find it in a bottle, a pill, or a cereal box. I'm skeptical that you can find it in a book on leadership . . . The truth is every good leader leads in his/her own way. Effective leaders start with their singular gifts and build on them."[11] Kellerman adds that "there is no top ten list of books whose supremacy and currency are self-evident," observing further that "leadership is contextual. What works in one era, setting, or organization simply doesn't apply to any other."[12]

Leadership ought not to be viewed, then, as some holy grail to be found or identified, once and for all. Rather, leadership needs to be embraced as more of a reality to be experienced and lived rather than only a discipline to be learned and studied. In essence, effective leadership is an art that regularly requires some combination of wisdom, knowledge, understanding, good judgment, discernment, common sense, and, of course, experiential and book-and-classroom learning.

Effective leaders are not satisfied with knowing only about the requisite "hard skills" of leadership. These kinds of leaders are committed to continuous learning that includes an understanding of the soft skills, behaviors, and perspectives essential for effective leadership. The fuel that empowers this kind of learning is often experiential and intuitive.

Again, leaders have their own set of skills they bring to their leadership assignment. Their leadership assignment has its own unique context. Both soft and hard skills in combination, then, influence the mix of how leaders lead.

The Importance of Soft Skills in Leadership

Early in my career I had the idea that leaders needed to be stoic, emotionally disciplined, and in control at all times, especially in front of the public. People who reflected emotion were to be viewed as weak leaders. However, as I have become more seasoned in my experience as a leader, I have come to realize that human emotions—grief, friendship, admiration, affection, love, humility—are what make us more relatable to others. I can no longer separate my feelings from my leadership duties. This is what happens when I embrace soft skills. Let me illustrate.

During one of our commencement exercises at Taylor University, we had the immense privilege of having Dr. John M. Perkins—a famous civil rights leader who had endured various kinds of difficulty, even brutality, during the early days of the civil rights movement—deliver the address. It fell to me to introduce this dear friend to our audience of thousands of students, parents, siblings, grandparents, faculty, administrators, and board members. I stepped to the podium in a state of hesitancy, wondering how it would be possible to do an adequate job of summarizing the life of this man who was at once a father, husband, pastor, patriot, teacher, author, social activist, and counselor.

I turned and cast my eyes on this noble human being, who at age eighty-five was still sharp-minded and bold-voiced. But as I looked at him, memories flooded back to me of how on February 7, 1970, he had been arrested by white deputies during a civil rights demonstration. The deputies had thrown him to the floor of the Brandon jail and had kicked him, punched him, stomped on him, and then left him bloodied, bruised, and broken, offering no medical help and not caring if John died in his cell that night. But instead of filing lawsuits and seeking revenge, this dear saint of God spent the next thirty years in all-out efforts of reconciliation among peoples of all races. He served on the boards of World Vision and Prison Fellowship. He started day-care centers, after-school programs, church outreach ministries, food banks, and employment training facilities. He wrote nine books that advocated love, forgiveness, cooperation, and fellowship.

I had a "John the Baptist experience" in that moment, feeling I wasn't worthy of lacing this man's sandals; yet, here I was sharing the dais with him and being given the honor of presenting him to our audience. A lump formed in my throat. Tears came to my eyes. How unfair it was that someone so gracious and loving had been treated so viciously, yet still was able to emerge with love and warmth for all people.

I was awestruck by his life. I was humbled by his strength. I was mesmerized by his stamina, will, and vision. I could not speak for several moments. Those in the audience resonated with my feelings and were quietly respectful of my loss of composure. No one spoke. No one fidgeted. No one got up and left. Finally, John smiled at me and nodded, and I lifted the microphone to my mouth and joyously welcomed him to our university and to the day's festivities. By my transparency, John knew and the audience knew my feelings, and no one thought any less of me for my moment of genuine, honest emotion.

There are, of course, multiple other examples of soft skills and their organizational impact. How people communicate with love is but one example. Fortunately, there are common understandings and abilities that mark what leaders do and how leaders do their work. The very best of leaders build off a foundation that includes a commitment to character, integrity, and love for people. How those common principles and tasks are carried out, though, actually depend, as Kellerman has observed, on the context and timeframe in which one does leadership. For this there is no simplistic formula, no clever equation. To the question, "How does one lead here, in this context?" the best answer may still be, "It all depends."

Business leaders continue to understand that hard skills are no longer enough: "Little value has traditionally been given to their so-called soft skills. . . . Now engineers are beginning to realize that soft skills . . . will make an individual developer more marketable in the future."[13] Another writer says it this way: "The most profound transformation in business . . . is the downfall of the barracudas, sharks, and piranhas and the ascendancy of nice, smart people with a passion for what they do."[14]

The former CEO of Rosenbluth International, Hal Rosenbluth, has reflected on the importance of soft skills in his leadership, particularly the role of intuition. Noting first the reality of the quantitative hard skills, he then made this telling observation: "But those aren't that important to me. In fact they might be a hindrance, because they would take away from my gut instincts. My body talks to me. It literally shakes. I know when we're going to lose a business or when we're going to be successful in an acquisition before we even start. The fact that I've met the people first tells me the outcome."[15]

One hurdle leaders must often overcome is their reticence to understand that the acquisition of soft skills is critically important for effective leadership, at all leadership levels. Paradoxically, they sometimes believe the opposite—that their responsibility is primarily to develop competence and mastery of the hard skills, believing that the acquisition of soft skills is primarily for others. Recent research has pointed out this contradiction.

For instance, when leaders were asked to select from choices for themselves between "training programs focused on competence-related skills (such as time management) and warmth-related ones (providing social support, for instance), most participants opted for competence-based training for themselves but soft-skills training for others." But as these researchers noted, "[P]utting competence first undermines leadership: without a foundation of trust, people in the organization may comply outwardly with a leader's wishes, but they remain much less likely to conform privately—to adopt the values, culture, and mission of the organization in a sincere and lasting way."[16]

Learning about soft issues and their importance in leadership is the focus of this book. First, I identify and then discuss a relatively small handful of primarily personal soft skills that are essential for effective leadership—knowing, of course, that there are many others. Some of the soft skills identified can be developed as behavioral competencies, even habits. Second, I want to identify other soft skills that need to be reflected in the organizational dimension as attitudes or perspectives to be embraced. In some cases, there is no hard and fast distinction between soft skill competencies, behaviors, habits, attitudes, or perspectives. They are interrelated, and seemingly all blend. No matter. The important point is to remember that whereas hard skills are essential for leadership, they may not be enough to create the culture that will likely allow for robust mission fulfillment. It will be the exercise of hard skills, in combination with the skillful deployment of soft skills, by competent leaders, that will likely make the difference in what makes people in organizations effective or ineffective.

How This Book Is Organized

This book is separated into two primary sections. The first section is intensely personal and focuses on soft skills that are essential for human functioning, and especially so for those involved in organizational leadership. These personal soft skills not only provide a foundation for living and leading, but also enhance and hopefully transform the leader. The second section, building on the first, focuses on essential soft skills that need to be an integral part of organizational culture in some way. While soft skills have personal application, embedding them within an organizational culture leverages and expands their impact. Organizations are more effective when both soft and hard skills are properly deployed together as part of the leadership agenda.

What is presented in the following pages reflects a distillation of perspectives and observations learned through reading thousands of pages and coupled with thirty-five years of service in president/CEO roles. That learning continues.

A quick word about what this book is not. You will not find much, if any, emphases on what leaders *do*. For instance, there is limited focus on leadership tasks and other leadership responsibilities such as strategic planning, strategy development, change management, organizational visioning, and the many other traditional tasks regularly included on the various lists of what leaders do. Their absence doesn't mean they are unimportant or irrelevant. Rather, the focus here will be on how leaders lead, and the kinds of soft skills that they regularly employ to powerfully shape leadership results in their efforts to optimize organizational effectiveness.

The aim in this effort is to be as practical as possible—and perhaps less theoretical than some would desire. Obviously, good practice emanates from sound theory. But those theoretical books and articles already exist and will continue to proliferate, primarily through the academic and scholarly world. Alternatively, this effort is to write impressionistically—again, using Kellerman's words, "as leadership," not "about leadership."

One more observation. All followers of Jesus of Nazareth, not just leaders, are called to reflect soft skills and behaviors such as spiritual growth, qualities of character, and the fruit of the Spirit (love, joy, peace, patience, kindness, goodness, faithfulness, gentleness,

THE IDEA OF THE BOOK

Hard skills, while necessary, are not sufficient to meet all of the expectations for effective organizational leadership. Soft skills are also essential. Because leaders differ in terms of their skill sets and personality types, and because leadership is carried out in widely different contexts, the soft skills leaders pursue and deploy will be different.

Leaders need to focus especially on two types of soft skills:

- One type, primarily focusing inward, are those skills that help to build the interior structure of the leader—the space that few people see but which is vital to help support and stabilize the external leadership effort. These types of soft skills include emotional intelligence competencies such as emotional self-awareness, self-control, and self-management.
- The other type of soft skills are those primarily embedded within and deployed throughout the organization. These include embedding soft skills in the organizational such as creativity, forgiveness, and love.

This book will help you begin the journey of soft-skill exploration, but by no means does it complete it. That

and self-control) in all that is done and said. All followers are called to prayer and dependence on the leadership of the Holy Spirit, not just leaders. The fact that there are no chapters on subjects such as the importance of prayer, or spiritual gifts, doesn't mean they are unimportant. Indeed, those subjects, as leaders live them out, are indispensable. The hope is that this emphasis will be evident in the chapters that follow.[17]

will be an ongoing journey of discovery and continuous
learning.

The context for this book—in essence, the leadership
laboratory that birthed it—includes travel to almost
one hundred countries, twenty-one years in university
presidencies, and a fourteen-year presidency with a large
New York City nonprofit. These collective experiences have
included communication with international leaders from
more than 140 countries. For some of those leaders, the
conversation has been intense, has lasted several decades,
and is still continuing.

Within the US, there have been hundreds of other
conversations with leaders within the collegiate and larger
nonprofit world over three decades, including thousands
of students. This ongoing learning has been supplemented
with extensive leadership literature reviews. Many of these
types of learning experiences have been structured; many
others have been anecdotal, impressionistic, and relational.
Taken together, they have provided the fuel that informs the
content of this book.

◆

Soft Skills

The Personal Dimension

CHAPTER 1

Protect Sacred Space and Enable Deep Thinking

"As soon as Jesus heard the news, he left in a boat to a remote place *to be alone.*"

—Matthew 14:13a

"After sending them home, [Jesus] went up into the hills *by himself to pray.*"

—Matthew 14:23

"Think on these things."

—Philippians 4:8 (KJV)

In the beginning, God created . . . sacred space. That's not the way most biblical texts read, but in a way, creating sacred space is what God did in His initial act of creating. He created beauty in a sacred place. Part of His intent was to establish this sacred place as something to be honored throughout all of the earth, within our understanding of time, within the human heart, and by extension, within the workplace. As a result of God's creative act, the entire earth is the Lord's, as are all of its inhabitants: "The earth and everything in it, the world and its people, belong to Him."[1] This is the reason we care for the environment, why we steward and care for our bodies as the temples of the Holy Spirit. Who we are and everything we do needs to be viewed as being part of the sacred. The planet where we live, the bodies we dwell in, and the places where we exercise our vocation are the fulfillment of our calling—all of these can be considered to be sacred spaces, created and nourished and held together by God Himself.

These topics are already addressed in multiple books and articles, especially in regard to care for the environment and also in regard to care for the body as God's temple. The concept of viewing the workspace as sacred space is less regularly addressed. That is where this chapter begins. The creation of sacred space within our homes, the workplace, and our workday is vital for effective leadership.

Sacred Space Defined

What more specifically is meant by the concept of sacred space (or white space, as some have called it)? Could it be a location, such as a church, synagogue, or temple? Of course. When we lived in New York, the workplace and 24/7 mindset were sometimes overwhelming. I had to find regular times and a sacred space where I could pull away and stop, in order to hear God's thoughts better amid the confusion of my own. Fortunately, right next door to my office was a beautiful Catholic church with a quiet sanctuary. This became a regular place of solace and refuge, and I regularly looked forward to my visits. Might sacred space be a memory of a cherished place in time, such as at a chapel on the Michigan sand dunes where I would frequently meet with a close friend to pray about the future? Yes. Perhaps a place in one's heart during a morning jog or swim? Of course. The movie *War Room* is a great example of one kind of sacred space—a place where one can pray and cry out to God.

Sacred space is that place where boundaries are placed in some way that allows refocusing of the mind and soul on a different agenda, a transcendent one rather than a transactional one—where

THE CHAPTER IDEA

Because leadership responsibilities are so varied and complex, the leadership agenda will sometimes drift, often becoming dominated by leadership reaction rather than by leadership intention. As a result, reaction often becomes the leader's default position. Effective leaders protect their time and seek space, so that the meta-issues they face can be processed in thoughtful and intentional ways.

Provision for "sacred space" within the work environment enhances reflective leadership capacities, and increases the likelihood that appropriate "thought work" will become an important part of the leadership journey. Sacred space can provide opportunities for leaders to connect to their spiritual or transcendent selves in ways usually not possible, given the rigor and demands of the daily schedule.

Leaders consistently need to embrace a way of working that allows them to think deeply about issues they face. If caught up in the whirlwind of perpetual reaction, they run the risk of living in the world of the mundane and operational, rather than reaping the benefits of being more strategic and intentional.

The concept of Sabbath (not its legalistic version) embodies the idea of sacred space, as well as the belief that personhood is more important than unending work performance. In essence, the Sabbath experience (or something similar) provides boundaries that preclude the 24/7 mindset.

"Heaven seems to touch Earth and we find ourselves aware of the Holy, and filled with the Spirit."[2] It is within that space that leaders often gain a vision for serving and leading. Without it, we risk getting caught up with the noise and busyness of life. As a bank president shared with me, "I am frequently most able to connect with the presence of God when in solitude and silence. . . . I am then (better) able to approach my spiritual, personal, and work life with a resolve that is quite clearly forged by God."

We often don't like boundaries, believing they restrict and constrain. Yet, paradoxically, it is the boundaries that give us freedom. Todd Henry says it this way: "The reality is that we are not capable of operating without boundaries. We need them in order to refocus our creative energy into the right channels. Total freedom is false freedom. True freedom has healthy boundaries."[3] Henry further quotes Joseph Campbell: "[A sacred place] is an absolute necessity. . . . You must have a room, or a certain hour or so a day, where you don't know what was in the newspapers that morning, you don't know who your friends are, you don't know what you owe anybody, you don't know what anybody owes to you. This is a place where you can simply experience and bring forth what you are and what you might be."[4]

Sacred space is often where vision is birthed, where it is nurtured, and where it flourishes. It's where we listen to the "still small voice" saying "over here—here's the way forward." This is foundational for leadership. In this context Stephen Covey references the inner side of leadership: "It is in this . . . area where the soul of leadership is best determined and developed. And both the public and private dimensions of leadership will be shaped by the kind of fire which is kept in this furnace."[5] Yet, attention to the importance of sacred space is noticeably absent from leadership literature.

So, how does diminution of sacred space marginalize leadership? Or, stated another way: How does protecting and nourishing its presence enable it? Why should leaders embrace this concept of sacred space as a soft skill essential for effective leadership?

The Benefits of Embracing Sacred Space

Leaders lead out of who they are on the inside. One writer has noted that the first challenge facing leaders "is a matter of how to be [leaders]—not how to do [leadership]."[6] To be sure, a leader sometimes needs to be part actor, particularly in difficult situations where people need encouragement. If what people experience on the outside, however, is not grounded by some kind of transcendent or spiritual depth on the inside, the leadership persona or façade will be eviscerated the first time an organizational storm is experienced. Ungrounded leaders without a strong inner foundation will likely fail. This will be addressed further in the next chapter.

Sacred space provides a better opportunity to understand and experience the presence of the spiritual in our lives—to understand that the source of our strength is not merely human, but also something from "the Lord, who made heaven and earth!"[7] The Bible repeatedly calls us to stop whatever else is occupying our time, to acknowledge God's presence in our lives. The psalmist's challenge to us is, "Be still, and know that I am God."[8] Isaiah's words amplify this point: "In quietness and confidence is your strength. But you would have none of it."[9] Like Isaiah's audience, many times we ask for God's wisdom in matters of importance but then rarely take the time to put ourselves in a position where we might optimize our ability to hear His voice.

Our human dilemma is that we often live life as if we know best. We study the issues, read the electronic and print literature, look at the facts, identify the opportunities, count the numbers, and then draw conclusions. All leaders have done this, believing in the rightness of their decisions. I count myself among them. But the reality is that leaders can't manage what they cannot know, nor can they lead if the destination is not clear. Oftentimes that is the leadership reality.

Fortunately, we serve a God who knows the alpha and the omega and everything in between. That's why Moses, acknowledging that he couldn't lead by himself, quickly concluded that if God was unwilling to go with him on his assigned leadership journey, he wasn't going. In other words, he wanted and needed God's presence on the journey: "If you don't go personally with us, don't make us leave this place."[10]

The leadership dilemma is that sacred space is often missing in the lives of leaders: "Interruption-free space is sacred. Yet in the digital era we live in, we are losing hold of the few sacred spaces that remain untouched by email, the internet, people, and other forms of distraction. . . . When walking from one place to another, we have our devices streaming from dozens of sources. Even at our bedside, we now have our iPads with heaps of digital apps and the world's information at our fingertips."[11] A colleague once referenced this as having "Google disease."

Intentionally setting aside time for sacred space, and then taking the time to occupy it, often provides unanticipated direction and blessing. But just setting aside the time for sacred space is not enough. Anne Morrow Lindbergh identified this problem as our continuing inability to be still: "The problem is not entirely in finding a room of one's own, the time alone, difficult and necessary as that is. The problem is more how to still the soul in the midst of its activities."[12] Henri Nouwen observed that for him to access sacred space, he needed to "kneel before the Father, put my ear against his chest and listen, without interruption, to the heartbeat of God. Then, and only then, can I say carefully and very gently what I hear."[13]

When we lived in Oregon with our young family, we wrestled with an important decision. We believed I was to continue graduate school at the doctoral level. I had already been accepted at two Big

Ten universities as well as at the University of Oregon, about a two-hour drive from where we were then living. This was pre-laptop or personal computer days. My wife Marylou and I regularly engaged in the typical cost-benefit type of analysis usually connected to these types of decisions. But we wanted more. We wanted to know for sure where God was in this process and not just to settle for the most affordable option.

George Fox University, where we were employed at the time, had a wonderful retreat center close to campus. So Marylou and I agreed—each of us, separately—to take a day at its small two-person lakeside retreat A-frame to attempt to discern God's direction for us. Cell phones were not a problem—there were none—and we didn't have to concern ourselves with much more than our Bibles and legal pads. We had each committed to a full day of Scripture reading, prayer, meditating, reflecting, and writing (not exactly in that order, of course). I took the first day and found the solitude to be exhilarating. Blue skies, the water, beautiful fir trees—could there be any place better for the task we had committed to?

When I arrived home, Marylou eagerly wanted to know where my decision process ended up. But believing that God doesn't lead His followers in opposite and divisive directions, we agreed to keep our "conclusion" points to ourselves until the other had the same opportunity to "be still" before God. So the next week, Marylou went and had a similar experience, alone, with pen and paper, her Bible, and time with God. She came back with what she thought God had said to her.

Paradoxically, we ended at opposite places. But after discussing the matter a bit further, we realized that our beginning assumptions were different. She wanted to follow God's provision of financial security through continued employment, whereas that was not my initial concern. I suggested that we at least needed to give God the opportunity to provide some alternative nonemployment funding, which He miraculously did. How? Shortly after these discussions, out of the blue, a person drove by our house and wondered if we would be interested in selling part of our small orchard, where a duplex could be built. Its ultimate sale provided most of the resources needed for further graduate schooling. Interestingly, it was the provision of stillness and solitude, along with the Spirit's direction, that eventually brought us to closure and a relocation.

Taking the time to experience sacred spaces such as the ones experienced at George Fox University seem to be exceedingly rare. Unfortunately, "despite the incredible power and potential of sacred spaces, they are quickly becoming extinct. We are depriving ourselves of every opportunity for disconnection. And our imaginations suffer the consequences."[14]

Azusa Pacific University has run a program for more than forty years called Walkabout, which provides sacred space for students in an intentional way. Primarily a wilderness program, it culminates in a "48-hour period of solitude, modified fasting, and spiritual focus—an intentional pause allowing students to seek the face of God and respond to Him. 'Students listen for God's voice and commit their lives to the year ahead.'"[15] The students from that program whom I talked to discussed both their initial apprehension about being totally alone with their thoughts and also the incredible blessing of extended self-discovery, coupled with a heightened awareness of God's presence in their lives.

Why should leaders embrace sacred space? "Solitude is one of the most important necessities of true leadership."[16] Solitude provides repeated opportunities for leaders to experience God constantly in their leadership, and often in different and innovative ways. Identifying and welcoming sacred space is, of course, not the only way for hearing God's voice, but it is often a part of doing so. But there is more.

Sacred Space Enables Deep Thinking

Deep thinking is the ability to think rigorously, extensively, comprehensively about any variety of issues important to leaders regarding a wide range of topics. They might be of a personal nature—as was our earlier referenced decision about graduate school—or they might involve multiple aspects of the organization served. Deep thinking, coupled with the counsel of colleagues, is often the source of new initiatives, new programs, as well as what Henry Cloud calls "necessary endings."[17] Deep thinking is sometimes interventionist in its nature, as it sometimes leads to a change in direction.

Sacred space and deep thinking are parts of the same continuum but merely located at different positions. They might be two separate events. When I develop the capacity for sacred space, I am setting boundaries. Deep thinking, too, requires boundaries. Sometimes deep thinking can take place within the boundaries set aside for sacred space, sometimes not. How I operate within or occupy that sacred space becomes an important choice.

When we were on sabbatical at Regent College in Vancouver, British Columbia, the Lord provided a beautiful home on the eastern slopes of Vancouver, overlooking the Cascade Mountains. On one side of the living room were two soft chairs that overlooked those mountains. Those chairs and the place where they were located became a sacred space for us, as we spent time, alone and with each other, in fervent prayer, shedding tears, and extended heart time while listening to God's voice. Interestingly, that's also the place where I authored another book on leadership.

The schedule of leaders is usually filled with meetings and appointments from the beginning of the day to often the late evening hours. So, here's the question: Where or when in the schedule do leaders take time just to engage in deep thinking? Maybe that doesn't happen. And if it doesn't, will leadership be effective?

William Deresiewicz talked about this in a widely circulated commencement address he gave at West Point. He noted that "true leadership means being able to think for yourself and to act on your convictions."[18] Commenting on the absence of leaders who can think this way, he then posed this question—in essence, every leader's question: "How do you learn to think?"[19] Further, where in the schedule of the leader is time provided for this kind of deep thinking?

Deresiewicz defined the ability to think not as multitasking but rather as "concentrating on one thing long enough to develop an idea about it."[20] That requires "slowing down and concentrating. . . . Thinking for yourself means finding yourself, finding your own reality." He continued by noting his concern with multitasking, that it actually impairs one's ability to think. He lamented the blogs, Facebook, Twitter, their progeny, and even *The New York Times*: "When you expose yourself to those things, especially in the constant way that people do now . . . you are constantly bombarding yourself with a stream of other people's thoughts. You are marinating yourself in conventional wisdom. In other people's reality: for others, not yourself. You are creating a cacophony in which it is impossible to hear your own voice, whether it's yourself you're thinking about or anything else." He then observed: "Leadership means finding a new direction, not simply putting yourself at the front of the herd that's heading toward the cliff."[21]

In three separate president/CEO employment situations, I had the privilege of serving boards who were sensitive to this need for deep thinking—we called it reflective leadership—and provided time throughout the year that enabled me to pursue it. I did something similar for our leadership teams. Providing opportunities for deep thinking is indispensable for leadership. Importantly, embracing the need for and engaging in sacred space experiences helps create the capacity to think deeply about the varied and complex tasks that leaders endlessly face. Without its provision, leaders run the risk of heading toward the cliff and falling off.

The Temptation to Be Busy

There are many who note concern for the busy schedules of leaders. Even though leaders are not necessarily any busier than many others, their busyness is often a result of an excessive workload or pervasive technology. Sometimes busyness can be a cover-up, an attempt to run from personal issues otherwise needing to be addressed.

I remember being on sabbatical in Vancouver, Canada, explaining to our pastor that while we wanted to be engaged in some kind of leadership role, we weren't sure we could be. This wise pastor simply observed that we didn't need to prove ourselves or our worthiness for this sabbatical. He could see beyond what we wanted to do and, instead, encouraged us to focus on what we needed to be. His gift of counsel freed us from our need to be "busy" on that sabbatical.

Busyness often is the curse of leadership. Nouwen notes that often our busyness tends to hide our need to know Jesus better. Sometimes we pretend our busyness is job-related. But many times, honesty compels us to admit that our busyness may only be a mask to cover up our need to address our innermost thoughts. So we stay busy, very busy.

Nouwen tells the story of a colleague who, with despair, was recounting "his hectic daily schedule—religious services, classroom teaching, luncheon and dinner engagements, and organizational meetings." Eventually, this colleague admitted, "I guess I am busy to avoid a painful self-confrontation."[22] Interestingly, Deresiewicz made a similar conclusion for the West Point cadets: "It seems to me that Facebook and Twitter and YouTube . . . are all ultimately just an elaborate excuse to run away from yourself. To avoid the difficult and troubling questions that being human throws in your way."[23]

I have participated in hundreds of leader-type gatherings where the usual discussions involve politics, legal issues, money raised, enrollments, sports, and the usual good news about the organizations they lead. Once in a while someone will mention something personal pertaining to his or her family. But the ever-present topic that often dominates the discussion is the "B" word—just how busy everyone is. Keeping up with social media management and email are usually prime concerns. Here again, the provision of sacred space as a soft skill helps establish a zone of protection, a type of boundary or safety net, against job busyness. Sacred space also provides a place where the "troubling questions that being human throws in our way" can be confronted and addressed.

We had to face that reality several years ago with our busy schedule. As a couple, we convinced ourselves that we only had time to deal with the hot-burner issues of life—the ones demanding immediate attention. We ignored those issues that were only simmering but, unfortunately, were the ones ultimately that might quietly emerge to the boiling point—issues that can cripple a marriage or destroy a workplace. Fortunately, we were able to embrace sacred space, which allowed for the presence of a gifted marriage coach who helped us work through potentially damaging issues that otherwise could have gotten lost in the busyness of our important work. Again, the provision of sacred space can be an appropriate antidote for the self-destructive "routine" of the busyness of life.

There is also the busyness of the workplace, especially for CEO-types for whom the expectation is that they will always be reachable, always within the reach of technology. My brother spent twenty years as a pastor, and pastors know this reality very well. While he was on a much-needed vacation, how could he say "I'm on a needed vacation" to a parishioner who just experienced a tragic loss? There is also the busyness that we self-impose from our often excessive need to stay connected, increasing the tension and competition between cyberspace versus sacred space.

In many ways, technology has enabled a new end, to stay connected, rather than a means to stay connected. And because of the presence of cell phones, iPads, and computers—all of which have excellent uses—this hegemony of pervasive personal technology simply dominates and pushes away other good things. For instance, and being honest, how many times do we check our phones for messages, new texts or tweets, or news updates? Every hour? More frequently? And to what extent does doing that diminish our focus? Many times as we end our day, rather than talking through our day, we reach for our smart phones to check the latest messages, news, or sports scores.

To illustrate this pervasiveness, how would we react to losing our cell phone for a day? A week? A month? For most, including me, it would not be a normal day or week, and I would go crazy trying to let everyone know about my loss, trying all the while to rectify it. One summer, my cell phone fell in a lake. I almost called 911. Within the hour I was rushing my "patient" to the nearby AT&T hospital where I was given this diagnosis: "pack it in rice for the next forty-eight hours." I felt lost for a couple of days before I once again experienced the "joy" of being able to reconnect with my mobile world. Often, if we're not in a position where others can interrupt our day, at any time, for any reason, we probably don't think we're being good spouses, parents, grandparents, citizens, or good leaders. These interruptions are exacerbated by the senders' or callers' expectation of a timely response.

I am not anti-technology, as I use it and benefit from it daily. Nor am I saying that it was "better" years ago. Actually, it wasn't. What I am saying is that if leaders are not careful, technology can completely dominate and obliterate any and every semblance of sacred space. This is why the management of busyness and technology becomes critically important. This is where the provision of sacred space and its use becomes relevant, essential, and pivotal for effective leadership. I want to encourage leaders to ensure the provision of sacred space so as to ensure their ability to ascertain and listen to God's direction and to enhance their capacity for deep thinking.

Honoring the Sabbath and Sacred Space

Making sure they have sacred space is foundational for leadership. If sacred space, which provides fuel for the leadership furnace, is nonexistent, then on what foundation will leaders build their leadership agenda? If there is no capacity to listen to and seek the voice of God, if there is no capacity for deep thinking, then what? How does one go about enabling the development of sacred space?

One way is to pursue the biblical concept of the Sabbath experience. There is a clear link between the concept of sacred space and the biblical concept of Sabbath. Early in the book of Genesis we find these words: "So the creation of the heavens and the earth and everything in them was completed. On the seventh day God had finished his work of creation, so he rested from all his work. And God blessed the seventh day and declared it holy, because it was the day when he rested from all of his work of creation."[24] It is not a far reach to substitute the word "sacred" for the word "holy."

The text notes that this seventh day was set aside as sacred or holy because it was the day God rested from all of his work. Given that an all-powerful God would not have been tired as a result of his multiple creative activities, why did he rest? Perhaps to serve as an illustration— as an example to us in our work? Clearly this seventh day was to be different from the others based on what God himself said about it.

Additional scriptures, particularly in the book of Exodus, add to what was meant by this concept of Sabbath rest or sacred space. Take the Ten Commandments, for example: "Remember to observe the Sabbath day by keeping it holy. You have six days each week for your ordinary work, but the seventh day is a Sabbath day of rest dedicated to the Lord your God."[25] This idea of a day of rest had application for servants/employees as well as for animals. Later, in Exodus 23, the purpose behind this focus on rest was referenced: "It also allows . . . you to be refreshed."[26] Rest and refreshment, too, are important parts of the Sabbath and part of what results from the provision of sacred space.

An additional reference in Leviticus identifies another purpose for the Sabbath day—sacred assembly: "You have six days each week for your ordinary work, but the seventh day is a Sabbath day of complete rest, an official day for holy assembly."[27] Whatever else might be its significance biblically, the scripture seems to present multiple purposes for the Sabbath day: cessation of our ordinary work, rest, and sacred assembly before the Lord. This, too, has application for our discussion of sacred space.

Clearly, this Sabbath concept calls for leaders to limit the amount of time spent on their ordinary work to only six days. Nowhere is there a declaration about any limit, one way or another, to the number of hours worked within those six days. But on the seventh day all of that work should stop—no 24/7 workweek for leaders, or their employees. The scripture clearly indicates that parameters are appropriate for our work schedule, for us and for our staff. Part of the reason for embracing sacred space is because it provides the kind of backstop to a 24/7 work mindset—again, illustrated through the concept of the Sabbath limitation of the ordinary work week to six days.

Oftentimes, in place of rest, I used the sixth and seventh days to catch up with all of the errands we neglected during the first five days, resulting in exhaustion, instead of rest. Further, in our work schedule, we often had multiple weekends filled with campus events. As a result, we sometimes arrived back to the office on Monday exhausted from a busy weekend. Pastors do not have the option of making Sunday their day of rest. But the concept would nevertheless apply—there needs to be another day where the day-of-rest concept can be honored.

These teachings about the Sabbath are convicting in yet another way. I think about all the work I removed from my desk and placed on the desks of colleagues simply by pushing the "send" button on my email on weekends. Leaders also need to be sensitive as to when that "send" button is pushed, as staff also deserve the restorative rest and sacred space leaders so often seek. Achieving effective rest is also part of developing the capacity for sacred space. As a result,

I tried as much as possible to avoid pushing the "send" key, in terms of giving colleagues work to do on weekends.

As mentioned earlier, the Sabbath concept includes sacred assembly. This, too, is part of sacred space. Why? So often those in leadership draw the erroneous conclusion that when it comes to the workplace, everything depends on the leader. Sacred assembly, to the contrary, helps reorient leaders in another way—to the sufficiency of God alone coupled with our need to be in community. He alone deserves our worship, and He wants us to walk in obedience to His ways. Sacred assembly helps dramatically reinforce that perspective. We have friends who recently retired from a college presidency who told us they arranged almost every Sunday to be in their home church with their nearby family.

In brief, the concept of the biblical Sabbath calls leaders to exercise the discipline of limiting their work schedules; emphasizes the importance of restorative rest; and highlights the necessity of relocation for sacred assembly, allowing us to refocus our attention on the God who established sacred space in the first place.

I want to emphasize that I'm not promoting some kind of Sabbath legalism as the solution for sacred space. What I am saying is that the principles regarding Sabbath provide guidance as to how we can work better to ensure the preservation of sacred space in our lives. Jesus reminded us that the Sabbath was not the end, but rather a means to an end: "The Sabbath was made to meet the needs of people, and not people to meet the needs of the Sabbath."[28] We need to avoid destroying ourselves by never stopping our work, neglecting our need for restorative rest, and by remembering that our work is seldom about only us. We need to be about honoring His work and His presence in our lives.

Author and speaker Skye Jethani gives us one more very practical reason to link sacred space and a Sabbath focus to our work: Sacred space allows us to be more productive.

PUTTING THE IDEA TO WORK

By insisting on having consistent and regular breaks to their work schedule, leaders are better able to achieve life balance. As a result, they can focus on issues and agendas over and above those they usually deal with. This includes the ideas of relocating from regular work space, and worship.

- Some leaders create space by taking a couple of days from regularly scheduled work outside of the office, and do so repeatedly every couple of weeks. Sometimes this includes a long weekend.
- Other leaders take additional weeks, perhaps over the summer, to engage in reflective leadership and deep thinking, in order to wrestle with strategic agenda items. My prayer during many of these times has been something like: "Lord, give me wisdom, knowledge, insight, good judgment, and common sense in abundance on these matters." Wise are the boards who insist that their executives regularly make time in their schedules for sacred space and deep thinking.
- In higher education, academic faculty regularly have access to faculty sabbaticals. With further study, that concept, perhaps in a modified from, could be extended more broadly to other arenas of activity.

Far from diminishing the value of our work, resting increases it. "Music," says composer Claude Debussy, "is the silence between the notes." It is the orderly rhythm of sound and silence that creates melodies and the soul-stirring music we cherish. Without silence, there can be no music—only noise. Similarly, our lives require a rhythm of work and rest for meaning. Without

regular periods of rest, our work loses it meaning and deteriorates into chaotic toil. What many of us have lost is a rhythm of
work and rest in a frantic pursuit of achievement. As a result, we
are making a lot of noise but very little music. Taking a day each
week to rest is more than a way to find rejuvenation. Sabbath
gives us the opportunity to step back from our immediate daily
demands to appreciate the fruit of our labor and to see our work
in the larger context of God's work. In other words, rather than
diminishing the importance of work, Sabbath frames and defines
our work so we can see its true value.[29]

To summarize, we need to ensure the presence of sacred space
and embrace its life-giving provision as a leadership soft skill foundational for leadership. Its provision provides us, as leaders, the
space to engage in deep contemplation, where we can think through
and wrestle with the multiple complex issues we face. Without
sacred space, we risk not hearing God's guidance for the journey. In
so doing, we—and the enterprises we lead—risk getting lost in the
weeds. Celebrating and protecting sacred space is an important first
step as we begin our soft skill leadership journey.

CHAPTER 2

Build a Foundation for Leadership

"It is like a person building a house who digs and lays the foundation on solid rock. When the floodwaters rise and break against the house, it stands firm because it is well built. But anyone who hears and doesn't obey is like a person who builds a house without a foundation. When the floods sweep down against that house, it will collapse into a heap of ruins."

—**Jesus of Nazareth**[1]

When Marylou and I lived in New York City, we would often take walks at night in our community to observe new building construction sites. Often, there was a barrier of boards that surrounded each one, but sometimes an opening was cut out forming a window so we could peek in, to watch what was going on below the surface and behind the scenes. What we saw was a hole—a very deep hole. The taller the building, the deeper the hole. It was in those deep places that the foundation was being laid that later would support, hopefully, buildings of fifty stories or more. Mostly unseen, the foundation was essential to the stability of the building that would result. The builders didn't begin the project by starting with the roof. Rather, the first step was to build the right foundation and then proceed up from there. Foundations give stability under pressure. If done correctly, they serve well in the midst of storms and earthquakes.

In the same way that buildings need foundations, so, too, do leaders. Leaders without foundations of some kind will topple and collapse in the midst of adversity. The writer in Proverbs states it this way: "If you fail under pressure, your strength is too small."[2] So what should those foundations for leaders consist of, especially if viewed as behaviors to be lived and practiced?

Stephen Covey, in *First Things First*,[3] illustrates the importance of foundations for leadership with a story about a seminar instructor, a gallon jar, fist-sized rocks, pebbles, sand, and water. The story begins with the seminar instructor placing the fist-sized rocks in the jar until seemingly full, and then asking the obvious question: "Is that jar full?" The quick answer was "yes," but then the instructor proceeded, in turn, to add in smaller pebbles, which easily fitted around the rocks; then sand, which fell through the cracks. Eventually, water was added.

When asked by the instructor to identify the point of the illustration, one answer given was: "Well, there are gaps, and if you really work at it, you can always fit more into your life." The instructor quickly responded: "No, that's not the point. The point is this: if you hadn't put these big rocks in first, would you have gotten any of them in?"[4] Covey then notes that "if we know what the big rocks are and put them in first, it's amazing how many of them we can put in. . . . [T]he key point is that the big rocks . . . are in first."[5]

"If we know what the big rocks are"? The use of the term "big rocks," and the need to "put them in first," are in essence metaphors for describing a leader's foundation. There are dozens of big rocks that arguably should be part of a leader's foundation.

The provision of the sacred space discussed in the previous chapter is surely one of those big rocks. Ensuring the provision of sacred space allows a place where leaders can wrestle with those "put in the big rocks first" kinds of issues, which allows them eventually to place first things first. The provision of sacred space ought to be viewed as a *sine qua non* for leaders.

Jesus emphasized the importance of establishing the right foundation (Matthew 7:26). He told His followers to build their foundations on the rock, not on the sand. The wrong foundation leads to collapse when the storms come. The right foundation leads to stability that will survive the tsunamis of life. Jesus noted that this foundation involves listening to His words and obeying what He was teaching.

So what are some of the other big rocks or braces that need to be part of the foundation out of which one does leadership—a foundation for leaders that will help keep them from drifting, to enable them to stay focused? I want to emphasize only a few in addition to sacred space, knowing, of course, that leaders will select from among many others as places to begin.

1) Ensuring a spiritual foundation is one of those leadership "big rocks."

2) The ability to ask the right question is another.

3) A determination to finish what you start, no matter what, is also essential.

A Leader's Spiritual Foundation

The Bible contains various teachings that can be viewed as providing a spiritual foundation for leadership. There are a couple of places that specifically speak to the issue of qualifications for leadership. These qualifications, when taken together, are examples of putting in the big rocks first.

Paul, in his letters to both Timothy and Titus, articulates what he views to be some of the big rocks of leadership. Interestingly, the majority of the qualifications he shares are soft skills, not hard ones. They include family matters, character and reputation issues, being hospitable, and the importance of setting priorities. Only one of the more than a dozen qualifications listed speak to biblical content—the requirement that the leader evidence spiritual maturity and not be a new convert. Importantly, all of these qualities are informed by many other biblical passages. They are grouped as follows:

Family

Several areas of focus are referenced. Moral purity, as evidenced by a healthy marriage (the husband of one wife) and the ability to manage well the home and family, is the place Paul starts. Indeed, because of the hard work required to achieve a healthy family, having a healthy family and marriage may be the initial place to look to determine whether a person is capable of leading elsewhere. The inference seems to be that if one gets it wrong in the family community, one may have difficulty in leading in other types of communities. Leaders need to view their commitment to care for their family as leadership laboratories where these qualities and soft skills so essential to effective leadership can be put to the test. Paul seems to be saying these are the places to look first when considering someone for a leadership role.

Some organizations view academic credentials, skill sets, and organizational experience as the places to begin the job interview process. Although not unimportant, they should not be the only places to begin the process of "who is qualified to lead."

Character

Character focuses primarily on the essence of a leader that goes beyond the purview of what the public sees, the part of the leader only God sees and truly knows. Character is ultimately about how God views a leader, not about what people know or think about the leader. Character is about the leader's thought life, and the activities he or she engages in when no one else is around. Of course, God always is around. Character includes identifying what Hebrews 4:12 references as exposing our "innermost thoughts and desires" and finding them to be God-honoring.

THE CHAPTER IDEA

Leadership doesn't exist in a vacuum. It needs to be connected to something that provides a foundation of stability, especially during times of storms and chaos.

Having some kind of faith commitment—for me, a Christian faith commitment—provides a stabilizing set of beliefs as that foundation. A spiritual foundation should include attention to the following leadership essentials:

- one's family
- personal character and reputation
- the ability to provide hospitality
- an appropriate level of spiritual maturity reflected in consistent discipleship.

Part of the leader's foundation needs to include the ability to ask good questions, at the right time and in the right way.

Leaders need to commit to finishing what they start, and to remain ever-vigilant and faithful to their leadership calling, especially during the hard times.

This is the kind of outcome illustrated by the fruit of the Spirit discussion referenced in Galatians 5:22–23—love, joy, peace, patience, kindness, gentleness, and self-control—and in the qualities referenced by Peter in his second letter[6]—moral excellence, knowledge, self-control, patient endurance, godliness, brotherly affection, and love. All are foundational elements of character. They shape the part of the leader where no one is watching. If the leader's character is properly developed and shaped by these qualities, then those character qualities will be seen in the workplace. Adversity of any type usually fleshes out and displays one's character more than almost anything else.

Reputation

Reputation is primarily about how the leader is viewed by people in the broader context, in the workplace and beyond. The foundational qualities that shape and inform the development of character are also the ones that help shape reputation. Having a good reputation within the family and beyond is an important leadership quality. Reputation includes being seen as a good role model, as well as having a lifestyle beyond reproach.

Since one's leadership task includes mentoring younger leaders, which is what Paul was doing with Timothy, entrusting a younger person to be mentored by the older one is an act of trust. If the reputation is sullied, that mentoring process will be jeopardized. Parents entrust their young people to their university of choice, believing that the university will build on the foundations they have worked hard to establish, and hoping that the university will help strengthen those foundations. Parents want and deserve to have those who teach their children to be persons who are teachable themselves, are of unquestioned character, and well thought of by others.

Being Hospitable

Having a good reputation also speaks to the issue of getting along with others in appropriate ways. This is also where hospitality comes in, as its primary focus goes beyond the needs of the leader to the needs of others. Sometimes one hears from leaders the comment in the workplace that "once I leave, that's my time." Interestingly, one qualification for leadership is that the leader be hospitable— that is, the leader recognizes and gives attention to the reality that people's needs go beyond the workplace. That attention also extends to the home as a place for hospitality. This too is part of authentic community and informs one's reputation.

Hospitality is more than a location. It is a mindset, an attitude of service and attention to the needs of others, regardless of the perceived "adequateness" of place where hospitality is practiced. Expressions of hospitality may look different, depending on one's locale and circumstances. Hospitality starts with one's family. To paraphrase Henri Nouwen, leaders need to see their children as their most important guests who come, stay for a while, who receive special attention, and then move on.

On one of our trips to Brazil, Marylou and I were on the Amazon River, helping with a ministry that was part of the Bible Society of Brazil. At one of the stops, Marylou was invited with several others to have a cup of tea in a small Amazonian hut. The hostess had placed flowers on the table in a gourd. She whacked away at a hazelnut with a machete and offered her guests its delicious meat. It was one of the best examples of hospitality Marylou has ever witnessed. Why? Because having almost nothing, this Amazonian woman shared with us everything she had. That is the essence of hospitality.

Again, being hospitable means that the focus is on meeting the needs of others. The needs of those being led have to be the leader's priority. Sometimes the best way to learn about issues that affect the workplace come from appropriate less formal or structured expressions of hospitality, when people are "off hours." Hospitality and its practice, according to Paul, are also part of putting in place a spiritual foundation.

Spiritual Maturity

There is the expectation that the leader ought to be mature in his or her faith. This is where the multiple spiritual disciplines are put to use, and where attention to "all Scripture" and its usefulness comes into play.[7] When leaders commit themselves to learning and living by being connected to these biblical foundations and disciplines, a life of faithfulness usually results. It is then that people see the growth and maturity so necessary in the lives of leaders and the organizations they serve. One mark of spiritual maturity is the ability to discern between right and wrong (see Hebrews 5:14). Discernment is not learned by following an operations handbook or procedures manual.

Leaders are also expected to reflect maturity in how they view money. Leaders are not to be materialistic or to love money. They must know the answer to the question, "So, how much is enough?" Spiritual maturity in matters of money allows leaders to embrace the joy of living a life of contentment and shared sacrifice. They understand that how they handle smaller amounts of money will likely determine how they would handle larger amounts. Jesus said it this way: "If you are faithful in little things, you will be faithful in large ones. But if you are dishonest in little things, you won't be honest with greater responsibilities" (Luke 16:10).

Spiritual immaturity results in greediness, and sometimes that can lead to both individual and organizational destruction. Sadly, the organizational leadership literature is littered with the stories of leaders who struggled in meeting this spiritual maturity expectation.

Each of the qualifications referenced in Paul's letters to Timothy and Titus speak to the spiritual foundation that is an essential qualification for leaders. These "big rocks" are necessary practices and behaviors and attitudes that leaders need to embrace and commit to as places to begin building their spiritual foundation for leadership. They help leaders and the organizations they lead to stay on course.

Ask the Right Questions

In addition to putting in the big rocks of a vibrant spiritual foundation, another important foundational leadership expectation is to know how to ask the right questions—the strategic questions—and when to ask them. Asking the right questions is a staple in the world of critical thinking. Perhaps the classic book, Browne and Keeley's *Asking the Right Questions: A Guide to Critical Thinking,*[8] is one of the reasons. But so too, the ability to ask the right question, the strategic question, is a necessary and foundational leadership skill (as John Maxwell has noted in his book by the same title, *Good Leaders Ask Great Questions*).[9]

In a board meeting where we were interviewing a potential board candidate, one of the observations made was that this person was especially qualified for board leadership because of her ability to "ask the right questions." This ability is not often included on the "qualifications for leadership" lists. Why is that ability foundational for effective leadership? If leaders and the organization focus on the right questions, the strategic issues, the organization stays focused. The leader stays focused. A simple clarifier by the leader as to whether an issue being considered is a tactical distraction or a strategic question pointing to an opportunity to be pursed is but one example.

Leaders engage in and lead many meetings. But before a meeting is convened, whether with an individual or a group, there must be an understanding in advance of the questions that need to be addressed and hopefully answered in that meeting. Patrick Lencioni further notes that there are at least two questions leaders ought to ask at the end of every meeting: "What did we just agree on at this meeting?" and "What should we all go back and communicate to our direct reports over the next twenty-four hours?"[10] Answers to those questions bring clarity and improve organizational communication.

When I was in law school, one of our professors constantly drilled us in learning this important priority. He would often pound the desk and repeatedly ask us, "So what is the issue in this case?" Often we students would be chasing rabbit trails related to less important issues. His point was that if we were identifying the wrong issue, or asking the wrong question, we would seldom, if ever, get to the right answer. So, too, in organizational life. Identifying the right issue, asking the right questions, identifying the strategic issues, are critical skills for leaders to help an organization stay focused and on mission. The ability to ask the right questions also qualifies as one of those "rocks in first" soft skills.

In our system of criminal justice, often the difference between whether the accused person is convicted or exonerated depends on the ability of trial attorneys to ask the right questions, at the right time. In organizational board meetings, sometimes the question that will clarify or define a given situation is the strategic question, regrettably often never asked. Professors and their students know the value of asking great questions.

This soft skill—asking the strategic question or asking the right question—was regularly modeled by the life of Jesus of Nazareth. He was always asking questions, and He often answered a question with another one. He was constantly asking His followers questions, dozens and dozens of questions. In multiple situations, Jesus did more than engage in conversation. He asked questions and patiently waited for responses. Patiently waiting for people to respond is part of asking the right questions.

Jesus asked His disciples, "Who do people say that I am?" and then used their responses as a platform for teaching. To one person who was sick, He asked, "So what do you want me to do for you?"—a seemingly obvious question. But Jesus wanted engagement. There was the question of the cleansed leper who returned to express his thanks—"Were there not ten lepers I healed? Where are the others?" Or of the women caught in an adulterous situation, "Woman, where are your accusers?" Of his challengers, He asked questions about where John the Baptist was from and whose likeness was on a coin, and when food was needed to feed hungry people, he asked "what" questions, not "how much" types of questions. To others He asked whether it was easier to say, "your sins are forgiven" or to say, "rise up and walk?" On the cross He asked His Father, "Why have you forsaken me?" To Peter, His poignant question was, "Do you love me?"

Why did Jesus ask questions? Since He was the Son of God, why didn't He just make declarative statements, recognizing that all of His words were truth? Since Jesus, fully God, knew in advance the answers to the questions He was raising, why was asking questions a part of His focus? There are many answers, of course, but strategic questions have a way of engaging people. And strategic questions often expose what is in the heart. Strategic questions require focus and formulation of answers. They force people to think for themselves. Strategic questions have a way of disarming and unmasking us. Presidents and CEOs sitting before news reporters also know that reality. Strategic questions ultimately bring clarity to issues. Asking strategic questions is a form of teaching and learning.

As a law student, many of our classes were in large lecture halls. Even if we came to class prepared, we dreaded being asked questions so we often polished our invisibility. Law professors had a way of teaching us when they asked us questions, and sometimes their questions exposed our shortcomings about what we still needed to learn.

When we were living in New York, I was often involved in working with the media. Media questions, while sometimes off-putting, also had a way of bringing clarity, not confusion, to sometimes muddled discussion of issues. Confusion resulted when I waffled on my answers. On rare occasions, a media person would provide her questions in advance, which I always preferred. That way I could prepare better and respond in more helpful ways.

Just as our Lord frequently asked questions of others, always with a purpose in mind, the ability to ask the right questions, the strategic question, is an essential leadership soft skill. Paradoxically, I have seen people end up in the wrong leadership assignment simply because they failed to ask the right questions of a prospective employer. "If I had only known. . . ."

What are the kinds of questions leaders should be good at asking? In the first instance, effective leaders ask questions that are contexted in ways that ultimately advance God's kingdom. In the second instance, effective leaders ask the questions that others can and desire to capably answer. What are the types of questions we need to be asking from a kingdom perspective?

Leaders often limit their leadership questions to primarily those that focus on organizational results. We tend to ask fewer questions about how the programs we're pursuing advance the kingdom. One publication by the Evangelical Council for Financial Accountability (ECFA) made this observation: "We measure bucks, butts, and buildings. More is better!"[11] We should be even more committed to asking kingdom faithfulness questions. Why? Because faithfulness moves us from only quantitative hard skill questions to qualitative soft skill ones. Paraphrasing Hoag, Rodin, and Wilmer: Do we appoint leaders who map faithfulness-focused strategies, or those who focus on financial "common path" strategies? Do we focus more on quantitative metrics or qualitative ones? Do we ask the questions and outcomes that target growing God's eternal kingdom or only those that grow an earthly one? Are we more interested in results or in righteousness?[12] One of our alumni made the observation that Jesus' words were not, "Well done, good and successful servant," but "Well done, good and faithful servant."

Jethani underscores the importance of asking the strategic question by focusing on several biblical examples. He notes two: the Exodus narrative where Moses struck the rock instead of following God's instruction to speak to the rock, and the Gospels' record of what is often referred to as the story of the "widow's mite."[13]

If the question asked in the story of Moses had been: "Did Moses get relevant results?" the answer would be yes, because the people were thirsty and now they had water. But was that the right question? Jethani says no, observing that the strategic question in this situation was this one: "Was Moses obedient to God's command?" The answer clearly was no, and as a result, Moses was precluded from ever entering into the Promised Land. God wanted obedience as the outcome. Moses settled for only a utilitarian relevant result, providing water. The outcome and impact on Moses—no Promised Land experience—was the result of his asking the wrong question. His question should have been, "What does God want in this situation?" Instead, Moses asked and then acted on another question, "What do the people want?" Asking the right question is imperative for leaders.

In Jethani's second example, the disciples were at the temple watching people giving their offerings.[14] As is often the case in our contemporary world, the focus was on those who were giving the largest amounts. Even in religious organizations, the names on buildings tend to honor those who have given the most. Jethani observes that the observers' question was, "How much did they give?" But that was not Jesus' question. Jethani notes that after the widow had given her two mites, Jesus reminded His listeners that she really had out-given the others. Why? Because His question was not, "How much did she give?" but rather, "How much did she sacrifice?"

Again, those are the types of questions leaders ask to determine whether or not a given program or response aligns with a kingdom value. As the ECFA article suggests, if leaders ask only results-based questions, they'll only get results-based responses. But if they ask whether or not a proposed initiative aligns with kingdom values, and it does, they'll likely reap God's favor—"Well done, good and faithful servant!"

In the same way, perceptive leaders also ask the questions people want to answer, yet often, those are the ones that they are never asked. When Fred Smith, a former member of the Board of Directors of *Christianity Today*, would mentor younger leaders, one of his responses was to encourage them to make sure "you ask good questions." And how might that happen, they would wonder? Fred's response? "Ask the question the person wants to answer."[15]

Too often leaders are asking the questions only they want answered, not the other way around. An easy example of this comes from the fundraising world. Most leaders are engaged with organizations that need gift income for their projects and operating margins. Organizations have their needs and are regularly approaching donors about helping financially meet the organization's needs, and donors respond. Often, however, the donor wants to answer a different question.

The question the donor ultimately wants to answer is whether or not there is strategic alignment between his or her personal mission and the needs of the organization's mission. When given that opportunity, the result is often the difference between a smaller five-figure gift for the annual fund as compared to a truly transformational gift that takes an organizational mission to the next level.

The opportunities for asking the questions people want to answer abound in every corner of an organization:

- There are, for example, organizational questions of those who serve: What are your dreams for this place? How can we make it a better place to work? What are we doing that we ought not to be doing? What should we be doing that we're not doing?
- There are also a multitude of personal questions: What can I do more of that will help you do your job better?
- There are hospitality questions: Can we do lunch or breakfast or dinner?

Each of these, and many others, are examples of questions that could be asked that people truly do want to answer. For leaders, this soft skill also requires sensitivity to asking the "who, what, when, where, how, and why" questions. There are process and content questions.

There are financial and direction questions. Developing this kind of "ask the right question" mindset is also a foundational soft skill.

Author Lisa Lai addressed these issues in a *Harvard Business Review* article, "Being a Strategic Leader Is about Asking the Right Questions." She notes five questions that every leader ought to be asking their leadership teams:

1) What are we doing today?
2) Why are you doing the work you're doing? Why now?
3) How does what we're doing today align with the bigger picture?
4) What does success look like for our team?
5) What else could we do to achieve more, better, faster?"[16]

As she concludes, "Being a strategic leader is about asking the right questions and driving the right dialog for your team."[17]

Finish What You Start, No Matter What!

Leaders desire to be culturally relevant. We live and work in communities where our children attend school and where we like our neighbors. We desire to be liked, to belong, and it hurts when we are attacked, be it from inside the organization or from without. We need to remember, though, that one of the leader's primary responsibilities—if not the primary responsibility—is to curate, protect, and enhance the organization's mission and values often preserved and handed down from preceding decades, if not centuries. The biblical record reminds us that there is a difference between relevance and faithfulness. As we noted earlier, Moses got this wrong; many times so do we. Finishing what we start is about several things, but to be sure, it is about walking in faithful obedience to God's calling, no matter how difficult. This is a qualitative commitment a leader makes, not a quantitative one. It's about heart resolve, not cultural relevance. It's about keeping your word, no matter what the cost.

Multiple biblical stories illustrate the tension in this area, but one of my favorites is found in Daniel 3. In this Middle Eastern story, young

PUTTING THE IDEA TO WORK

Some leaders believe that family relationships and difficult matters affecting the family can—and ought to—be kept separate from work. That's mostly impossible. Turmoil and stress in the home affect performance at work. If there is respect and integrity and joy at home, that likely will carry over to the workplace.

Healthy families at home contribute positively to healthy performance at work. Organizations that recognize this put programs in place to help build healthy families, which also helps build strong and healthy organizational communities.

Leaders who wish to be known for their integrity in the business world need to move beyond simply engaging the business literature. They also need to explore the scriptural texts that provide wisdom and guidance, both personally and for their families. The Proverbs, for example, reference the need for wisdom, knowledge, understanding, good judgment, common sense, and discernment. These competencies are needed in both the personal/family world and the organizational one.

men were taken against their will to a foreign country, presumably from Jerusalem to Babylon, from Israel to Iraq, a place with dramatic cultural and religious practices far different from their own homeland experiences. These young men excelled in learning the language and literature of their new culture, and based on demonstrated differences, they were successfully granted the option to follow a diet different from that of the culture. Additionally, because they had so impressed those in political leadership with their demonstrated distinctiveness

Leaders who move into leadership roles should understand that their primary purpose is to serve both the mission of the place they serve and its people. They need to focus more on what they give to their communities than on what they get out of it. They also need to take the time to get to know the people they serve.

◆

The soft skill of learning to ask great questions is critical for effective leadership. Meetings should not start until there is clarity about the issues and/or questions that need to be addressed. Meeting follow-up questions are just as important, questions such as "So what was decided" and "How do we communicate what we decided to our direct reports?"

◆

Mission achievement and fulfillment takes time. While longevity is seldom a guarantor of success, there is seldom success without longevity. That's especially true for senior leaders.

in their knowledge and understanding—"ten times better than all the others"—they were given senior leadership appointments in the court of the king. From this auspicious beginning, however, they eventually realized that to be biblically faithful, they often had to live counter to their culture.

Babylon, like many contemporary cultures, had religious priorities. The king was at the center of the nation's religious practice, setting its priorities. A large statue was constructed by the king and all within the kingdom were commanded to worship it whenever the sounds of specified music was heard. It was a mesmerizing rhythm. The president of Fuller Seminary has referred to this music as the "mesmerizing rhythms of the culture."[18] The consequence of disobedience was dire—death in a fiery furnace. How did these three young men respond, having fully adapted to their new culture and having been given important positions of authority?

They recognized the situation for what it was—the challenge to be culturally relevant or to be biblically faithful. Because they had a solid spiritual foundation and asked what God expected of them in that situation, they respectfully declared their unwillingness to respond as the king desired, refusing to bow to the culture—in this case, the king's idol. They were willing to pay the price, and I paraphrase their response: "We know, O king, that our God has the power to deliver us; but even if He doesn't, we will never bow to your god."[19] Fortunately, for them, and to the astonishment of the king, they were delivered in the fire. First, though, they were willing to pay the ultimate price, death, to be biblically faithful, not knowing what the ultimate result would be.

Globally, persecution abounds for thousands of persons because they practice their faith in hostile environments. Whereas statues of gold are not being constructed, there are multiple mesmerizing cultural rhythms being sounded that call us to bow and worship what the culture deems relevant. We now see these concerns evidencing themselves more and more in the West. Just as in the days of this Babylonian story, contemporary leaders and the organizations we lead are being challenged to subrogate biblical faith to cultural relevance, with primarily negative financial consequences (fines, loss of government dollars, loss of employment) to those who resist.

Oftentimes leaders compare and contrast the difficulty of their leadership assignment with someone else's, asking a question something like: "Why couldn't that have been our leadership assignment?

At that organization, they never have had to deal with any of the things we've had to deal with here." The simple answer is: That is asking the wrong question.

As leaders recognize, leadership assignments are seldom the same. Jesus' encounter with Peter in John 21 illustrates this. Peter, who had previously denied Jesus three times, was involved in a conversation in which Jesus was sharing what Peter's future might look like. Upon hearing it, Peter almost immediately shifted into comparison-and-competition mode by asking Jesus about John's future— "So what about him, his future?" Again, the wrong question. Jesus' answer was in effect, "If I want him to live or die, what is that to you? You follow me!"

I once heard the story of a long-term missionary who had faithfully served in India. One day, during the monsoon season, he happened to be reading his university's alumni magazine. He was focusing on all of the promotions and achievements of his former classmates and immediately held his own pity party. In essence, he was asking, "Why can't I be famous and important like all of them?"—again, the wrong question. As the missionary tells the story, God interrupted the party with these words: "You are to focus on the depth of your walk with me; I'll take care of the breadth of your walk with me."

God often calls the person He has equipped to stand in the gap needing to be filled. Those gaps are seldom identical. Compare, for example, King David's assignment with Solomon's. Compare Moses' assignment to that given to Noah, or Ruth's assignment to Esther's. What was always expected was for each to finish what was started—faithfulness, not success, at least not in the way that term is usually defined.

That takes us to Jeremiah, whom God called when he was in his late teens.[20] As a prophet, Jeremiah's message was extremely unpopular: Tell the people of Judah that God would no longer defend

Jerusalem; and that they should, therefore, submit to God's punishment, which was exile in Babylon. His message, "stop resisting the Babylonian armies," sounded like treason. He was rejected and threatened by the religious and political leaders.[21] Jeremiah understood the difference between difficulty and impossibility, so he was determined to be faithful and to finish what God had called him to do.

Part of finishing what you start, part of being faithful, is also referenced in Ecclesiastes: "Finishing is better than starting."[22] One of the ways culture has squeezed into many organizations is through the mindset of leaders that "I can leave my job for greener pastures anytime I want to—no matter the word I may have given on an employment agreement, no matter the harm caused to the organization through my departure, no matter the poor timing." It is particularly important that senior leadership keep their word in these kinds of situations, as the fallout can be very damaging to the organization and its people currently being served. I need to be a person of my word, and keep my word through the employment arrangements I make, not walking away simply because I have found a better situation.

In my first college presidency, I was closing in on ten years of service and the board awarded us a sabbatical which took us to Regent College in Vancouver, BC. While there, I was approached by another organization with a very enticing offer. It was, however, not a good situation for our family, and we didn't consider it seriously. Several months later we were approached again by the same organization, in essence offering the same opportunity but with a start date of a couple of years later. Though better in terms of timing for our family, the problem was that I had a sabbatical service commitment that I would have to break if I pursued that opportunity. I didn't want to break my word, and I was committed to finishing the work I had been hired to complete. So, what to do?

I explored the new opportunity, but only with the understanding that my current board would need to willingly release me from future employment obligations. Years before, a mentor had taught me that there are always two sides to God's call—a call to and a call from. I needed to respect God's leading on both sides, not just on the "call to"; both sides needed to honor the timing. I remember the board meeting where this issue was raised. The motion put to the board was this: "All in favor of releasing Gene and Marylou to be missionaries to the world, say Amen!" The tearful decision of "yes" was unanimous. That was a powerful, emotional, tearful moment for us as it underscored the importance of both a "call from" as well as a "call to."

Part of a commitment to finishing what you start also involves keeping your word in what you have been called to do. The higher the level of responsibility, the more important that commitment becomes—and the more harm that will result if you don't honor it.

To summarize: God's call to lead requires that leaders recognize their need to build a foundation for their leadership that includes spiritual depth and breadth. This foundation needs to include multiple areas of emphasis. But it should clearly include building a spiritual foundation. Leaders need to learn the clarifying skill of learning to ask strategic questions. And, leaders must also determine to be faithful in their calling—to finish what they start, no matter what the difficulty or crises or the temptation to go elsewhere. It is this kind of foundation for leadership that enables soft skills to flourish at home and in the workplace.

CHAPTER 3

Welcome Self-Discovery Learning

"Anyone who stops learning is old, whether at twenty or eighty. Anyone who keeps learning stays young."

—Henry Ford[1]

"The future belongs to the learning, not to the learned."

—Mary Louise Rowand[2]

"In times of change learners inherit the earth; while the learned find themselves beautifully equipped to deal with a world that no longer exists."

—Eric Hoffer[3]

Leaders who commit to a lifestyle of continuous learning engage as learners in multiple dimensions. David Lidsky notes in *Fast Company*, "The best leaders are sponges, absorbing impact, inspiration, and ideas from a large and varied set of sources before choosing their path forward."[4] As a result they are constantly improving themselves, and motivating the people in the organizations they lead to do the same.

Sometimes I am asked, "When did you decide on the career goal of being a university president?" They are surprised when I state that it was never a career goal. The goal instead was to pursue a quality-of-preparation goal—to complete all of my formal education by the time I was thirty-five, along with having ten good years of a meaningful workplace experience. Thereafter, I wanted to be a continuous learner, regardless of career choice. I believed that if I prepared well, reflected excellence in my work, and kept growing continuously, opportunities would find me. My focus was employability security, not job security.

Leaders who embrace continuous learning become students of themselves, God, the organization, and, of course, those they lead and serve. Part of continuous learning also includes getting to know the people you lead and serve. The movie *The Blind Side* illustrates this priority.

In the movie, the coach was repeatedly frustrated by his inability to teach his hoped-for star player how to block his opponent. Frustrated, the player's mother (played by actress Sandra Bullock) strode over to the field, past the coach, and did a quick instructional lesson for her son. She told him that blocking, and protecting those behind him, was like protecting his family, something he was already committed to. Instantly he understood his task because she shared a family story he could relate to. After observing the instantaneous difference, the pleased-but-perplexed coach wanted to know what she had said to her son. Her response is instructive: "Burt, you've got to get to know your players better." So, too, must we. That, too, is an important dimension for continuous learning.

Various pieces of literature note the need for leaders to be learners. For instance, representative writings from the ancient apocryphal book of Sirach, the Psalms, and the Proverbs say it this way:

> I have always been a learner and am grateful to everyone who has been my teacher. . . . Come to me, all you who need instruction, and learn in my school. Why do you admit that

you are ignorant and do nothing about it? Here is what I say:
It costs nothing to be wise. Put on the yoke and be willing to
learn. The opportunity is always near.[5]

I am eager to learn all that you want me to do, help me to
understand more and more.[6]

And if you live right, education will help you to know
even more.[7]

If you have good sense, you will learn all you can.[8]

Many in the business world have noted the importance of continuous learning as an important skill for a leader. Tim Sanders, writing in
Fast Company, notes, "To be an impact player in business, you simply
have to know more than most other people know. That means taking
the power of ideas seriously, reading books voraciously, and developing
a system of organizing what you've learned."[9] Professor Noel Tichy of
the University of Michigan Ross School of Business observes, "Leaders listen, and they are hungry to learn."[10] Harvard professor Richard
Chait gives an example of the need for people to be learners in a particular direction. He observed this about a weakness of then-Harvard
University president Lawrence Summers: "Summers will have to learn
to speak with a softer voice and to be . . . a charismatic listener."[11]

It is likely that leadership success, both current and future, will
be determined more by the learning that takes place after being
given a leadership assignment than by what has been learned prior
to it. While past learning may have gotten leaders their position, it
will be their future learning, in multiple areas, that will help keep
them there. Again, it is not that past learning has become irrelevant;
it's simply no longer enough.

Organizational Learning

For instance, one type of learning in which leaders continuously engage is the pursuit of knowledge that leads to organizational

THE CHAPTER IDEA

For leaders, a willingness to continue learning is a normative expectation. Why? Because the future belongs to the learning, not to the learned.

What is learned after the leadership role is accepted will likely matter much more than what was learned prior to it. There are several types of learning important to leadership.

- One type is *organizational learning*—learning about things like organizational history, its people, its accreditation reports (for a university), current strategies, and its goals for the future.
- *Individual learning* may or may not be of direct benefit to the organization. But if it is of benefit, it is considered to be a form of organizational learning and worthy of organizational budget support.
- *Self-discovery learning* includes the idea of learning directed at understanding one's self, one's motivation, and individual strengths and weaknesses. Many are oblivious to their impact on the organization, for better or for worse. Many leaders are unaware of their blind spots and are unwilling to address their weaknesses. Self-discovery learning helps leaders become more authentic and more self-aware.

improvement. The author of *Clear Leadership*, Gervase Bushe, notes the importance of "the outcome of an inquiry that produces knowledge that leads to change."[12] Inquiry-based learning that leads to the acquisition of knowledge is one type of learning. But in the context of the organization, unless it leads to organizational change of some kind, it may not be enough.

In the university world, for example, faculty members have the opportunity to apply for sabbaticals—extended time away from normal classroom and teaching assignments. The sabbatical focus is to encourage continuous learning in the direction indicated by Bushe, learning that somehow will also bring benefit to the university. Among other benefits, the results of sabbatical learning could be improved programs and learning opportunities for students. Bushe's point is to challenge leaders to differentiate between the learning that makes one a better person and the learning that leads to organizational change. It is not a far stretch to conclude that learning that makes someone a better person will also likely produce some kind of organizational change. Obviously, both kinds of learning are important.

One more observation about organizational learning: To be effective, all the three components previously referenced need to be in place—inquiry, knowledge, and change. "All three components have to be present for an episode of organizational learning to take place. Knowledge that doesn't come from inquiry is revelation, not learning. Knowledge that does not lead to change might be called conceptual learning, but without practical results it's not organizational learning."[13]

I have found that leaders have to be excellent students of the organizations they lead. For example, they need to know about the organization's history, its past leaders, and especially about how issues have been addressed and solved. Sometimes the seeds for change in the future can be found in the way issues were addressed in the past. Sometimes histories also provide clues as to what should be avoided in the future.

Self-Discovery Learning

To focus only on organizational learning, however, is not enough for leaders, nor is it the primary focus of this chapter. Leaders also need to become skilled at self-discovery learning—that is, learning about themselves, usually not an eagerly sought-out assignment. Since one leads out of who one is and not the other way around, self-discovery learning is critically important learning. This became clear to me in a previous leadership assignment.

I was working with a colleague who was having a difficult problem with a direct report. As he gave me the blow-by-blow recitation of the issues he was dealing with, he stopped short, sort of shuddered, and then said something like this: "Here's another thing: All that touchy-feely stuff, I don't get it." Neither do a lot of other male leaders, and neither did I at one time in my life. Women often appear to be much more willing than men to go deeper into this area, the world of feeling self-discovery. Many men would rather learn almost anything else than about their feelings.

Some leaders tend to focus learning almost exclusively on getting the desired results, or the "what" of the leadership assignment: assignments such as getting the budget balanced, the buildings built, the products sold—basically, getting the job done. They have a relentless focus on organizational learning, which is an important focus, to be sure. And why not, since that tends to be the focus of the assigned bottom line and the reward system?

Unfortunately, many times employees are called upon to clean up the organizational carnage, and sometimes have to pay the ultimate price of job loss that results when leaders are less than aware about "how" their methods have adversely impacted their employees or have otherwise damaged the ethos of the organization. Self-discovery learning gives attention to these and other matters. Leaders who are willing to do the heavy lifting of self-discovery learning—including better understanding of their strengths and their weaknesses—usually discover and evoke more authenticity, more honesty, and more humility in their leadership.

The emphasis on the soft skill of self-discovery learning is hardly a new focus. Unfortunately, it is often ignored. For instance, the pages of the Bible have stated these "soft" expectations for centuries. The followers of Jehovah, and later Jesus of Nazareth, were instructed: "Love the lord your God with all of your heart, soul, and mind. This is the first and most important commandment. The second most important commandment is like this one. And it is, 'Love others as much as you love yourself.' All the law of Moses and the Books of the Prophets are based on these two commandments."[14]

The expectation is to love the transcendent—"the Lord your God"—and further, to love others as we love ourselves. One is a vertical expectation, the other a horizontal one, but both expectations are built on an understanding of self. It is on these points that we leaders often fail, as we simply don't know ourselves well enough. That is, we don't know our hearts and motivations, nor do we know well enough the individuals we are privileged to serve.

In the Sight and Sound theatrical version of "Moses," the main character has been chased from his power position in Egypt. Years later, when confronted by an Israelite slave critical of his leadership behavior, Moses retorted, "You don't know who I am," playing the power card. But the rejoinder to Moses was brilliant: "No, you don't know who *you* are."[15] So often this is the leadership dilemma. Leaders often don't know the ones they serve, nor do they know themselves.

Frederick Buechner emphasizes this point in his book *Telling Secrets*: "Life batters us in all sorts of ways before it is done. . . . The original, shimmering self gets buried so deep that most of us hardly end up living out of it at all. Instead, we live out all the other selves, which we are constantly putting on and taking off like coats and hats against the world's weather."[16] Leaders are not immune to these realities. Buechner suggests we sometimes pretend to know ourselves, but do we really, and are we even making the effort to find out?

I wish I had pursued this kind of effort earlier in my life, both personally and professionally. For instance, I can remember a very specific situation in which I was so bruised and battered by a particular leadership issue that I had functionally abdicated my presidential leadership assignment to an outside consultant. I remember walking around the block, complaining all the while about this to Marylou. Finally, she looked at me and simply said, "You need to go back upstairs and be the president." I had to take note of what I was running from, face the fear, and with God's help, go back into that situation and lead with renewed courage.

That experience, and others, subsequently led us to engage a marriage coach—a trained professional who could help us engage in self-discovery learning in our coupleness, to be more authentic in both our work and personal lives, and with each other. We call this kind of self-discovery learning preventive maintenance for our marriage. Self-discovery, in this way and others, is vital for leadership. Sometimes we need help to discover who we really are.

The esteemed business writer Chris Argyris, former professor emeritus at Harvard Business School, spoke of an earlier time in his life when he thought he was doing excellent leadership, only to find out that in reality he was only being tolerated: "[W]hat was relevant was how unaware I had been. That's what got me started learning more about myself and my own blind spots."[17]

All leaders have blind spots we reluctantly admit to and acknowledge. Sometimes we simply ignore them. We leaders need to be honest with ourselves and with our leadership teams about where those blind spots exist and where help is needed. Interestingly, Marylou and I have found that each of us is uniquely equipped as a spouse to speak into the other's life. We've also discovered that sometimes we need a third party to help us either to build bridges or tear down walls. Leaders need to work hard at staying in touch with themselves, their abilities and inabilities, and thereafter, at building a team around them to compensate for those gaps. Pursuing "360-degree feedback," where the leader invites a variety of people to speak into and evaluate his or her performance, along with other similar tools can be helpful in that regard. These are all examples of self-discovery learning.

Richard Semler, owner of a Brazilian company, notes the reality that every CEO's team observes daily: "Managers overrate knowing where they are going, understanding what business they are in, (and) defining their mission. It is a macho, militaristic, self-misleading posture."[18] Laura D'Andrea Tyson, former dean of the London Business School, notes that the lessons she learned from Robert Rubin include "the importance of recognizing one's own strengths and weaknesses" and that "a leader gets respect through humility, not arrogance."[19]

Former Clinton Treasury Secretary Robert Reich expands this "need for awareness" to include areas outside the workplace: "By all means, become more aware about what's truly important to you. Many of us know more about how we're doing on the job than about how we're doing in the rest of our lives. Off the job, we're not nearly as sure of what's expected of us or what we should expect of ourselves. We may have a vague and uneasy sense of what's lacking, but how do we recognize what doesn't exist?"[20]

Success in the workplace doesn't always translate to success in other areas of interpersonal relationships. There is not always a correlation between leadership position, money, success, and, if married, marital happiness. Although one might have all of the perks and the rewards of a leadership position, that doesn't provide insurance against having an unhappy home life, nor does it provide an automatic ticket to personal fulfillment.

The business magazine *Chief Executive* courageously featured a story on the problems of CEO alcoholism and the workplace. It noted that one of the reasons this kind of problem goes on for so long, unaddressed, is that sometimes CEOs refuse to be honest with themselves, and refuse to make themselves vulnerable enough to get help: "Not surprisingly, the stereotypical images of addiction fail to line

PUTTING THE IDEA TO WORK

- Leaders need to welcome and surround themselves with people who can honestly assess and provide feedback on their performance.
- Leaders need to embrace practices such as 360-degree reviews and other types of assessments, in which individuals and groups provide helpful performance insights.
- Once leaders become aware of their blind spots, they need to address them by learning new behaviors and/or by embracing strategies that limit their adverse impact.
- Leaders need to avoid leading in ways that get high performance scores but which do not take the organization in the needed direction.
- Leaders need to model and champion both organizational and self-discovery learning for their colleagues.

One place to start self-discovery learning is to read the history or histories of the place where they work, including their organization's foundational documents. Organizations are inextricably tied to their histories, for better or for worse, and histories inform not only possible future directions but also pitfalls to be avoided.

Another basic form of self-discovery learning for leaders is to pursue psychological self-assessments. I have found these to be personally helpful.

up with self-perceptions of successful corporate leaders. . . . Many CEOs want to be viewed as models of decisiveness and as being as totally together as possible, so it's very difficult for them. . . . CEOs, isolated by power and position, have a relatively easy time conceal-ing their addictions. . . . It is always lonely at the top. How is a CEO going to find anybody to talk to when he's drunk. . . ? The CEO then becomes more isolated, which gives him or her more room to engage in that substance abuse."[21] Alcohol addiction may not be every lead-er's issue, but there are other addictions, such as being a workaholic, pursuit of pornography, or abusive relationships.

This emphasis is made not to be judgmental or to point fin-gers, but rather to encourage more self-awareness, and to encour-age leaders to be more diligent at staying connected to objective reality rather than only a subjective reality of their own making. Not actively pursuing self-discovery learning, not being self-aware in as many areas as possible, limits one's capacity to take corrective action. If not addressed, it will become the source of a significant leadership Achilles' heel.

Henri Nouwen talks about the difficulty of this kind of self-discovery, noting that to pursue it aggressively is frightening, "as if the house I had finally found had no floors. . . . It seemed as if a door to my interior life had been opened, a door that had remained locked during my youth and most of my adult life. . . . The interruption . . . forced me to enter the basement of my soul and look directly at what was hidden there."[22]

To be sure, honest self-examination, especially for leaders, is not easy. It can be downright scary for the uninitiated. We'd rather keep our busy schedules, doing important things, pursuing our organizational agenda. All in senior leadership know that reality; we've all been there. Nouwen suggests that one of the reasons for the busy, seemingly frenetic schedules we leaders maintain is not driven by the necessity of the leadership position. Rather, we keep up that kind of schedule because it allows us to hide from ourselves, or from our spouse or children, or perhaps to escape the kind of positive introspection so necessary for life itself:

Many people who say how much they desire silence, rest, and quietude would find it nearly impossible to bear the stillness. . . . When all the movements around them have stopped, when nobody asks them a question, seeks advice or even offers a helping hand, when there is no music or newspapers, they quite often experience such an inner restlessness that they will grab any opportunity to become involved again. . . . [I]t is indeed not surprising that vacations are more often spent on busy beaches, camping grounds, and around entertainment centers than in the silence of monasteries. . . . We are so afraid of open spaces and empty places that we occupy them with our minds even before we are there. Our worries and concerns are expressions of our inability to leave unresolved questions unanswered and open-ended situations open-ended.[23]

Our busyness frustrates our ability to pursue honest self-discovery and self-awareness. We simply don't take the time to do it. All leaders know this frustration and reality. When Marylou and I were on our last sabbatical, she threatened to give me an "F" in Sabbatical because I found it very hard to detach from work in the way Nouwen describes it above. Fortunately, I was able to go through busyness detox and was eventually able to benefit from the sabbatical, but make no mistake, it wasn't easy to stop being busy.

Stopping being busy may be extra-difficult to those who feel called to life-saving tasks, whether those tasks are physical ones or spiritual ones. I was reared in the church that sang hymns with words like "rescue the perishing, care for the dying" and sometimes I convinced myself that it would be sinful if I ever took time to stop and rest. In addition to resisting rest to avoid inward self-examination, leaders sometimes resist rest due to the urgency of their mission. We need to remember that the Son of Man completed everything He was called to do in three years, yet He regularly took time to rest and pray. So, too, must we.

In our leadership, we are not well-served if we simply don't regularly make efforts to better understand the need for self-discovery learning. We not only miss the opportunity to know ourselves better, but we lose the opportunity to envision an alternative future, a potentially clarifying vision that could be helpful for informing a new organizational vision:

> Our preoccupation helps us to maintain the personal world we have created over the years and blocks the way to revolutionary change. Our fears, uncertainties and hostilities make us fill our inner world with ideas, opinions, judgments, and values to which we cling as precious property. Instead of facing the challenge of new worlds opening themselves for us, and struggling in the open field, we hide behind the walls of our concerns holding onto the familiar life items we have collected in the past.[24]

A quote usually attributed to Soren Kierkegaard states, "It is good once in a while to find oneself in the hands of God, and not always slinking around the familiar nooks and corners of a town where one always knows the way out."[25] While accepting the validity of this point, I nevertheless want to resist it. Yet, leaders are often called to walk in unfamiliar places and carry out undesirable tasks.

One of the most unfamiliar and difficult leadership decisions I've had to make was to close down a campus—knowing that it would affect the lives of hundreds of faculty, staff, and students. I wanted to run from this decision or defer it so someone else would eventually have to make it. But the decision had to be faced and made. At another time, two days before my inauguration, a tragic accident took the lives of five persons within our campus community—and then five weeks later, we learned that two of those persons had been misidentified.[26] Compared to the grief of the affected families, our load was small. Again, these too were times where all of us were driven to trust God in new ways and to let Him lead. There simply was no other way. Unfamiliar? Definitely! Undesirable? Clearly! Spiritually stretching? Absolutely!

As noted earlier, organizational success does not guarantee personal happiness and does not assure marital or familial contentment and fulfillment. Writing in *Business Life*, James Oliver referenced a *Forbes* survey about a decade ago of the four hundred wealthiest people, a list that included several leading CEOs. Oliver observed:

> [T]he most fulfilled and mentally healthy are by no means the ones on the top floor with the biggest offices and most share options. . . . A sharp rise in our aspirations and individualism . . . has led to an all-consuming preoccupation with our status, power, and wealth relative to others. We compare ourselves obsessively, enviously, and self-destructively, corrupting the quality of our inner lives.
>
> The result (with regard to marriage) is an unprecedented "gender rancor" and divorce rate, a holocaust of broken bonds at precisely the point in history when we are demanding more from our relationships than ever before. We are addicts searching for a fix of . . . intimacy, but ironically, it is the breaking of passionate attachments that is the greatest single source of despair.[27]

One of the reasons this may happen is that one spouse simply outgrows the other. When I was a student in law school, for example, the phrase constantly used by professors was that "the law is a jealous mistress." Students were told upfront that because of that, there would likely be divorces after graduation as a result. Our encouragement is that, if married, each spouse needs to pursue self-discovery learning concurrently, so as to mitigate against one spouse outgrowing the other and as a strategy to strengthen marriages.

Ironically, often the messiest divorces are the ones of the otherwise highly successful CEOs we regularly read about in the news. And whereas leaders can handle multimillion- or multibillion-dollar company budgets, they sometimes have no clue as to how to manage themselves or their relationships—especially those that depend on their love, as with a spouse or children. Perhaps one of the reasons has to do with their inability or inadequacy or unwillingness to do self-discovery learning, to deal with their interior landscapes and what goes on within. So, as Oliver has observed, leaders end up corrupting the quality of their inner lives, all the while denying that reality. What happens? Leaders run, to another spouse, another corporation, another community.

Ken Gire makes this observation about unpursued self-discovery: "[I]f the soul is somehow shut off from God, shielded from the sunshine of its eternal significance, it will seek its significance elsewhere, sending out its roots in search of the right job, the right school, the right organization to join, burrowing deeper, thinking if it gets enough money, enough power, enough prestige, it will satisfy its longing for significance."[28]

Earlier in this chapter I referenced Gervase Bushe, particularly his discussion about inquiry that results in learning that leads to organization change. He also weighs in on this topic of self-discovery learning, observing that many leaders refuse to pursue personal self-discovery, running from almost any effort to acquire this kind of soft skill competency. But then, he explains why: "Most . . . do not describe what is going on in themselves. It doesn't seem like a natural thing to do. This tendency does not necessarily come from malicious intentions, fear, distrust, or any other negative reason. It is just that we have never been taught to do so. Some people are even taught not to do so."[29]

Many leaders don't know what's going on inside them—and even if they do, often don't know how to interpret that activity: "We are constantly pulled away from our innermost self and encouraged to look for answers instead of listening to the questions. . . . Unless our questions, problems and concerns are tested and matured in solitude, it is not realistic to expect answers that are really our own."[30]

Leaders who embrace the soft skill of self-discovery learning must take the time to know themselves to the core. They relish the opportunity to pursue self-discovery. They recognize that "they are effective because of who they are on the inside—in the qualities that make them up as people. They understand that to achieve the highest levels of organizational leadership, they need to understand themselves better. They need to develop soft skills from the inside out. If you can become the leader you ought to be on the inside, you will become the leader you want to be on the outside."[31] In other words, leaders who understand their interior landscape, including their problems and addictions, their strengths and their limitations, will likely become better leaders. Nouwen counsels us to "acknowledge your limitations, but claim your unique gifts and thereby live as equals among equals."[32]

One of my staff members who modeled this kind of self-discovery served with me in Oregon. He would regularly take retreats with his wife, and together they worked with a mentor. At the time it all seemed rather mysterious and unnecessary to my way of thinking, particularly since they were practically newlyweds. But he was modeling for me and the rest of our staff this reality of self-discovery learning, of being in tune with one's interior landscape.

To summarize: The opportunities for new learning are without end—be it interior learning, organizational learning, or some kind of purposeful cognitive learning. Things I have found particularly helpful have included professional conferences and pursing in-depth experiences. Several that have been particularly beneficial to me were a month-long intensive Institute at Harvard; a semester-long "scholar in residence" experience at Regent College in Vancouver, British Columbia; and a week-long senior management experience in Quebec with the American Management Association. Other possibilities include online classes and dedicated time for a robust reading schedule in selected areas of needed discovery. An immersive Spanish language experience in South America is another.

The safe thing to do is to try nothing different, nothing new. Who relishes the risk of failure of attempting anything new, particularly as they get older and/or are given more organizational responsibility? So we play it safe, staying comfortably within our castle walls of sameness, perhaps dying a bit each day because we've settled for the same old, same old. Paradoxically, the safe option of staying the same increases both personal and organizational risk. Why? Because knowledge is continually expanding, and the world is continually changing. Playing it safe in this area puts one on the highway headed toward obsolescence.

Self-discovery learning is essential for effective leadership. Leadership tasks are too complex, the organizational dimensions too political, and the people realities too unpredictable for authentic leadership to be carried out without establishing first an interior foundation based on self-discovery and self-knowledge, coupled with a sense of transcendent hope. Not much else matters if we don't get this inside focus right, no matter our leadership experience or inexperience. Self-discovery learning is a crucial element to achieving this.

Stephen Covey wrote extensively on the interior space of the leader—the part of us that no one else sees, or maybe no one else even knows about. Yet, for leaders, "Both the public and private dimensions of leadership will be shaped by the kind of fire which is kept in this furnace."[33] "Each of us guards a gate of change that can only be opened from the inside."[34]

Leaders committed to self-discovery understand how to open this personal gate of change. In so doing they optimize the probability that they will end up living more meaningful lives while leading and serving more effectively, whether at home or in the workplace.

CHAPTER 4

Stay Connected to the Heart

"As a face is reflected in water, so the heart reflects the real person."
—**Proverbs 27:19**

"The work of the eyes is done; now, go and do heart-work on the images imprisoned within you."
—**Rainer Maria Rilke**[1]

"[B]ut once I had brains, and a heart also; so having tried them both, I should much rather have a heart."
—**L. Frank Baum,** *The Wonderful Wizard of Oz*[2]

"It is the heart, not the head, that guides us through the world."
—**Skye Jethani**[3]

Healthy self-discovery learning is one way leaders stay relevant. Because the outside world, organizational environment, and people are constantly changing, the feedback the leader gains from this kind of learning helps ensure the organization and its leadership will remain on the same page. Often, the organization that was being led ten years ago is not the same organization it is now. The temptation for leaders is to "freeze" what they know about leadership and then move that frozen paradigm into the future. That obviously doesn't work. Self-discovery learning that is dynamic, not static, enables the leader to be more in touch with critical organizational change. It has been said that an organization has got to "change a lot to stay the same." It needs to change even more if it wants to advance beyond staying the same. The same principle applies to people.

One way that happens is by staying connected to the heart. Yet for many, embracing the soft skill of heart-work is uncharted territory. Most likely staying connected to the heart does not dominate many executive lunchroom conversations. Why is it that we tend to be more comfortable exploring the external, "hard" realities of our world? Why, for instance, do decisions based primarily on intuition tend to make us less settled, less certain? Why is it that we often tend to be more comfortable with decisions based on notebooks filled with charts, tables, graphs, analytics, and statistics suggestive of a decision in one direction rather than another?

The reality is that many leaders never let their followers see this part of them. Yet, the leader daily operates in this sphere of the heart. The Proverbs say it this way: "Guard your heart above all else, for it determines the course of your life."[4] Having the right kind of heart and staying connected to the heart is another soft skill and it is a foundational focus for leaders.

What Does It Mean to Focus on the Heart?

The focus on the heart is part of what some have referred to as the "being" side of leadership. "Being" pertains less to what leaders do and more to who leaders are. The being side is contrasted with the doing side. Interestingly, what we do is informed by who we are. Being precedes doing. Frances Hesselbein, former chairman of the board of the Peter Drucker Foundation, says it simply but powerfully:

"[L]eadership is a matter of how to be, not how to do it," noting that in the end, "it is the quality of character of the leader that determines the performance, the results."[5] And how does one focus on being? By keeping connected to the heart.

Here again is another area where I have had to grow. My entire background has focused more on the development of the mind and on the thinking, rational parts of my life rather than on relating to matters of the heart. To be candid, at one stage of my life I often looked at those whose lives were primarily driven by matters of the heart as maybe not tough enough to be effective leaders. How wrong I was. I have observed that I was not alone in this type of thinking.

Whereas care for the heart is a popular subject in some circles, it is regularly dismissed in others as quaint, if not irrelevant. When we lived in New York City, I remember walking into the local Barnes and Noble bookstore where I purchased a book entitled, *How to Become CEO: The Rules for Rising to the Top in Any Organization.* Here was its first rule: "Always take the job that offers the most money. . . . [G]o to work for the company that offers you the most money. . . . In business, money is the scorecard. The more you make, the better you're doing. Simple."[6] There was no emphasis on the need to assess the job requirements or whether the job was a good fit when compared against one's personal giftedness; no consideration of the needs and desires of one's spouse or family; no assessment of the extent to which a given job will produce joy or gladness in the heart.

Unfortunately, one of the reasons organizations sometimes get into trouble is because their leaders, and perhaps their boards, make money matters the primary bottom line. Not the mission, not the ethics or values; not the customers or constituents; just the money. It's often all about the money. No wonder employment statistics regularly show significant percentages of people who are unhappy in the workplace, not enjoying their jobs. In those kinds of organizations, employees end up serving only as paycheck recipient mercenaries rather than being passionately connected to a larger mission and vision.

Compare the "go to work for the company that offers you the most money" approach to the counsel of another, Frederick Buechner: "The voice we should listen to most as we choose a vocation is the voice that we think we should listen to least, and that is the voice of our own gladness. What can we do that makes us the gladdest, what can we do that leaves us with the strongest sense of sailing true north and of peace, which is much of what gladness is. . . ? I believe that if it is a thing that makes us truly glad, then it is a good thing and it is our thing and it is a calling voice that we were made to answer with our lives."[7] It is the heart that pulls me toward this intersection—where my gladness and the needs of the world meet.

When I was in graduate school, Marylou and I were contemplating our first full-time positions. I was headed to university work, and she to public school teaching. I had several job offers, so I decided to seek the counsel of the professor I was then studying with. His counsel, never forgotten, was not to take the job with the most prestigious university nor the one that paid the most money. Rather, his counsel was to take the job where I could learn the most, the one that would give me the best opportunity to get more deeply involved, the one that would allow me the opportunity to continue pursuit of learning opportunities apart from employment. It was great advice that I followed, and it proved to be true.

In the culture at large, on the one hand, people hear the siren call to money and success. Yet, on the other, their hearts seem to be calling them to something else, perhaps something better. Robert Reich aptly identifies this cultural tension: "We hear a rising chorus of . . . voices resolving to slow down. Yet more of us seem to be speeding up. We say with ever more vehemence that we value family. So why are our families shrinking and family ties fraying. . . . We talk more passionately than ever about the virtues of 'community.' And yet our communities are fragmenting. . . . The problem is that balance between making a living and making a life is becoming harder to pull off because the logic of the new economy dictates that more attention be paid to work and less to personal life."[8]

Michael Volkema, former CEO of Herman Miller, also notes this tension: "I think society has told us to compartmentalize ourselves, so when we show up for work, you're supposed to leave fatherhood behind; leave motherhood behind. . . . Never again will I separate who I am from what I do, and never will I let what I do become who I am."[9] The former CEO of Baxter International, Harry Kraemer, echoes Volkema: "I want people to bring their whole person to work. Baxter should be sensitive not just to people's work lives . . . but also to their family, community, religious, and health concerns."[10]

Working only for money? Nothing could be further from staying connected to the heart. Volkema and Kraemer have the preferred balance. They know who they are. But do we know who we are? How do we get our hands around this dilemma? How might staying connected to the heart provide insight?

Staying Connected to the Heart—Some Perspectives

There have been many writers who have helped us on this point. David Allen is one, with his book *In Search of the Heart*.[11] John Eldredge is another, especially with his books *The Sacred Romance*[12] and *Wild at Heart*[13] In addition, we have appreciated the writings of Henri Nouwen, Madeleine L'Engle, and also a seventeenth-century mystic by the name of Francois Fenelon, particularly his book *The Seeking Heart*.[14]

The Scriptures make the matter of the heart the priority emphasis. Jesus of Nazareth confronted the religious leaders of His day over many issues and concerns. One of those concerns was their preoccupation with an external agenda rather than having first a proper focus on an internal agenda. A primary example of this focus is recorded

---

THE CHAPTER IDEA

Focusing on "heart leadership" is more about the leader than about leadership. Heart work is more about what goes on inside of the leader that heavily influences the outside work of leadership—the part people see.

Heart leadership is both a psychological and spiritual term. It speaks to perspectives like fear and sadness, but also to joy, centeredness, and gladness.

Being heart-connected allows people to consider other life realities when making the initial employment decision— things like, "Where can I learn the most?" "What is best for my family?"

Organizations that celebrate heart-connectedness welcome colleagues who celebrate the importance of whole persons and healthy families.

When hearts are fully and healthily engaged in the workplace, both individuals and organizations are more fully protected from the ravages of a militant and potentially destructive self-interest.

---

in Matthew 23:28: "Outwardly you look like religious people, but inwardly your hearts are filled with hypocrisy and lawlessness." The writer of the Proverbs says it this way: "Guard your heart above all else, for it determines the course of your life" (Prov. 4:23).

This is one of the points made by Allen: Because our hearts are so important but also are filled with the wrong kinds of things, we have no room to focus on the kinds of things that produce goodness and beauty: "Our challenge is to become missionaries to our own hearts. So often we forget the painful feelings buried deep inside us—anger, fear, guilt—and the experiences that led us to feel that way. The heart is the repository for those painful feelings, but like a sponge it can only absorb so much emotion. Once it's saturated, there's little room left for love and joy and beauty."[15]

Eldredge calls us to make sure that "the Christian life is a love affair of the heart. It cannot be lived primarily as a set of principles or ethics. It cannot be managed with steps and programs. It cannot be lived exclusively as a moral code leading to righteousness. . . . Throughout [the Scriptures], the life of the heart is clearly God's central concern."[16] Because the culture at large doesn't give much attention to the heart, "we agree to give our heart a life on the side if it will only leave us alone and not rock the boat."[17]

There is this ongoing conflict with culture, especially because there are so many cultural references to the heart. For instance, "We describe a person without compassion as 'heartless' and we urge him or her to 'have a heart.' Our deepest hurts we call 'heartaches.' Jilted lovers are 'heartbroken.' Courageous solders are 'brave hearted.' The truly evil are 'black hearted' and saints have 'hearts of gold.' If we need to speak at the most intimate level, we ask for a 'heart-to-heart' talk. 'Lighthearted' is how we feel on vacation. And when we love someone as truly as we may, we love 'with all our heart.' But when we lose our passion for life, when a deadness sets in which we cannot seem to shake we confess, 'my heart's just not in it'."[18]

The reality seems to be that when issues become serious—whether personal or organizational, family or workplace—when all of the usual strategies and tactics have failed, we finally turn to heart words to better understand what we mean to say and to say what we mean. In organizational life, there are frequent events and ceremonies that bring us together as family, to laugh and cry together. National tragedies also provide living examples of this as the nation suddenly turns to talking about God, prayer, and matters of the heart. What leader hasn't used heart expressions or metaphors in communication where loss and disappointment are realities? But shouldn't the essence of the heart be the central focus all along? Why do we often wait until later, when we're in trouble, to deal with matters of the heart? "In the end, it doesn't matter how well we have performed or what we have accomplished—a life without heart is not worth living. For out of the wellspring of our soul flows all true caring and all meaningful work, all real worship and all sacrifice. Our faith, hope, and love issue from this fount as well."[19]

To paraphrase Eldredge, authentic leadership flows out of the heart that's right. If the heart shapes life, and if the heart shapes leadership, there will be more joy in the leader, more joy on the journey, and more joy in the family and in the organization.

As a leadership couple, we have been growing in this area of letting those we lead have access to our hearts. Marylou usually leads the way. It actually comes quite naturally for her, but it has been more difficult for me. I am growing. For example, I find myself more willing to express my emotion when I'm in front of people. There was a time when that wouldn't have happened.

We were also pretty transparent in front of our campus community as we shared from our hearts about our life journeys. We shared a careful selection of some of our struggles, but we also included examples of where we have benefited from counseling and from having a marriage coach. Sharing this journey to our hearts has made us more vulnerable to those we lead.

One evening after spending time with a campus couple, we were greeted the next morning with an email that read something like this: "Thanks for sharing with us so honestly last night. You helped save our marriage. Thanks for modeling for this community that it is okay for people to get help. We've already scheduled an appointment with a marriage counselor." We've learned that this kind of authenticity in leadership, especially at the heart level, builds bridges of mutual understanding between leaders and followers that rarely occurs otherwise.

Madeleine L'Engle illustrates yet another benefit of engaging the heart, not just the head, in leadership. In a commencement address at Smith College, she developed the idea that the greater good to be pursued was self-abandonment rather than self-fulfillment. She suggested that one's heart will be a type of sentry to guard and protect against preoccupation with self-fulfillment: "[T]he paradox is that the only sure road to freedom and true personhood is self-abandonment. . . . Think of the people you know who are the most fulfilled, the most free, most whole—I doubt if they waste time worrying about self-fulfillment. 'Self-fulfillment' widens the rift between the mind and the heart; the heart does not know how to think in terms of self-fulfillment; the heart is made for love."[20]

Our hearts are kind of like a safety net, a kind of self-corrective protection against self-fulfillment. But oftentimes, here's where we get into difficulty. What if we don't listen to the heart and listen only to the mind? What if we simply override the heart, ignore the heart? This appears to be a problem, as evidenced by multiple colossal business failures. Nouwen argues that the mind alone is inadequate to protect and provide certainty: "When the answer to our world remains hanging between our minds and our hands, it remains weak and superficial. . . . Only when our mind has descended into our heart can we expect a lasting response to well up from our innermost self."[21] Eldredge likewise notes:

[A] "loss of heart" best describes most men and women in our day. . . . There is the busyness, the driven-ness, and the fact that most of us are living merely to survive. Beneath it we feel restless, weary, and vulnerable. Indeed, the many forces driving modern life have not only assaulted the life of the heart, they have dismantled the heart's habitat—that geography of mystery and transcendence we knew so well as children. . . .

Starting very early, life has taught all of us to ignore and distrust the deepest yearnings of our heart. Life, for the most part, teaches us to suppress our longing and live only in the external world where efficiency and performance are everything. We have learned . . . that something else is wanted from us other than our heart . . . that which is most deeply us. If we are wanted, we are wanted for what we can offer functionally. If rich . . . our wealth; if beautiful, for our looks; if intelligent, for our brains. . . . We divorce ourselves from our heart and begin to live a double life. So we live the "external story of our lives" because that's the story we are known for best. And it's in our external story . . . where we carve out the identity most others know.[22]

All of these realities became painfully evident to us during the events of September 11, 2001. We were living in New York City at that time and witnessed the carnage of terrorism and its aftermath during those horrific days. Thankfully, there were many examples of heroes. While there were clear exceptions, the corporate sector did not always lead the way in terms of responding to and meeting the human needs of that awful event. Some corporate leaders, not all, were ill-equipped to meet the exigent heart needs that quickly emerged. Loss of life, the pain of loved ones and neighbors, the uncertainties of life—these and other issues were not initially addressed well by the application of a corporate strategic plan. Needy people—and all of us were, and still are—were calling for leaders to reach out to meet needs with their hearts. Those corporate teams that did respond well did so likely because they were informed by their hearts more so than by their heads. They willingly extended a heart response to human need.

How does one prepare for experiences like 9/11? None of us could even imagine in our worst nightmares what resulted. So what do you do? You respond through your heart, especially reflecting the heart of Jesus.

Our first priority became caring for our families, and our staff. All of the hurt experienced by families and neighbors came to the forefront. All of the despair and hopelessness caused by loss was at the top of our minds. That drove the response. We reached out to our communities, especially the first responders, including the New York City police and fire departments. Then we shifted to the broader needs of the city, focusing on the hundreds of thousands who were walking past our Broadway offices in shock. We began to prioritize the needs of the children, because of lost or injured parents. Throughout all of our efforts we emphasized hope—hope that comes through understanding God's heart and His love for people in these kinds of situations.

More than a decade after that event, we visited the 9/11 Museum downtown. It was a highly emotional event for us, and in some ways was disappointing. One disappointment was the limited focus the museum placed on the efforts of the various faith communities. Those communities contributed significantly to addressing the needs of the hearts that were hurting as a result of that tragedy.

The fallout from the multiple business failures of recent decades—too numerous to mention—will be debated and analyzed by the academic and political pundits for years to come. Could one reason for corporate failure be attributed to an uncontrollable bent toward self-fulfillment in the worst possible way? Might it be that these business failures were inextricably linked to heart failure, that is, that the people involved became totally disconnected from the values of the heart—substituting instead values such as power, greed, and control?

Again, the words of L'Engle bear repeating: "Self-fulfillment turns out to be imprisonment. And it widens the rift between the mind and the heart; the heart does not know how to think in terms of self-fulfillment; the heart is made for love." Staying in touch with the heart can be a powerful deterrent against self-fulfillment run amuck.

PUTTING THE IDEA TO WORK

Leaders need to work at getting connected to their hearts, using a variety of sources including:

- prayer, meditation, reflection, and journaling
- assistance and guidance from gifted counselors, coaches, or spiritual advisors
- reading and reflection on carefully selected books and articles
- choosing to be in touch with people and situations involving both beauty and pain
- pursuing spiritual literature—especially the Bible, as it has much to say about the heart

As heart work is done, focus more on asking "what" questions, not just "why" questions. Rather than asking "Why did that happen to me?" focus more on questions such as, "So what can I learn in this situation? How can I grow?" The shift in type of questions will move the questioner in the direction of the heart.

But staying in touch with the heart may not happen intuitively. Special and sometimes extraordinary efforts need to be made for heart work to become a reality in the lives of leaders.

How to Touch the Heart

Leaders need to be in touch with their hearts, to listen to their hearts, and to allow their hearts to both inform and protect. How is that to be pursued or addressed? How can leaders cultivate this important and necessary part of life? Reading books and asking lots of questions is a start. Getting in touch with a spiritual director or counselor is another.

I got my start when in the midst of working with our marriage coach, he shocked me with this question: "So what do you want?" The lawyer in me took over so I cleverly responded with "with regard to what?" His response was that he wasn't going to do my work for me and that I needed to get in touch with my heart to find out how I would eventually answer his question—"So what do you want?" He had asked me the right question. That may seem like a simple question, but it is also a profound one, one that requires heart work for its answer.

Being in touch with both pain and beauty also powerfully shapes and influences the heart. The first, pain, we try to avoid at all costs; the second, beauty, we seldom take time for. Eldredge quotes Simone Weil on this point: "There are only two things that pierce the human heart. One is beauty. The other is affliction."[23] Fenelon challenges us in these ways:

> Embrace the difficult circumstances you find yourself in, even when you feel they will overwhelm you. Allow God to mold you through the events He allows to enter your life. This will make you flexible toward the will of God. The events of life are like a furnace for the heart. All your impurities are melted and your old ways are lost. . . . The intrusions that God sends you will no doubt upset your plans and oppose all that you want. But they will chase you toward God.[24]
>
> Don't bargain with God to get out of this mess in the easiest, most comfortable way. Embrace the cross. Live by love alone.[25]
>
> You can see God in all things, but never so clearly as when you suffer.[26]

The Hebrew Scriptures present a similar picture. We learn from Job that "hard times and trouble are God's way of getting our attention."[27] We find story after story about the constant difficulties faced by the people being led and by their leaders, Abraham, Jacob, Joseph, and Moses, along with Esther, Judith, Rahab, and Ruth. Yet, the promise from God was not deliverance *from* difficulty but deliverance *in* difficulty. Pain to pain. Not plan and solution, but God's presence. We want the plan for deliverance but oftentimes marginalize the importance of God's presence. Here's how Fenelon makes this point: "Pray for strength and faith enough to trust yourself completely to God. Follow Him simply wherever He may lead you and you will not have to think up big plans to bring about your perfection."[28]

This is what Moses had to learn. In Exodus, we find Moses having completed the first phase of his leadership assignment. He had led the people out of Egypt. Thereafter, God provided the next assignment: "Now, get ready to lead them to the land I promised their ancestors."[29] Moses asked for a bit more clarification about the assignment: "[L]et me know what your plans are, then I can complete the assignment."[30] God's answer? "I will go with you and give you peace." No other plan, just God's presence. That would be enough. No promise of freedom from pain or difficulty, just His presence and promise.

Often, we in leadership are no different. We want deliverance from the difficulty, not deliverance in the difficulty or pain. We seldom welcome a major budget shortfall, the need to reorganize or change, handling difficult and sticky personnel issues, and a host of other difficulties. But it is often in these heart-wrenching situations that we have the best opportunities to demonstrate heart relevance to those we serve.

All in leadership have experienced these realities at one time or another. Ann Mulcahy, former CEO of Xerox, notes, "When you're in a leadership position, there's nothing like a crisis to help you focus. In many ways, it actually helps you lead and inspires others to rise to the challenge."[31] This is what we're talking about when referencing heart leadership.

We had to face (and continue to face) this kind of pain several years ago when I was diagnosed with two types of cancer in the very same year. It was obviously not something we welcomed or sought. And it produced many tears. But embracing the reality of the need to have two different types of cancer surgery, having pain be our teacher, and letting staff and family reach out to us in different ways, was truly life-changing. It truly impacted our leadership style. It gave us time to catch up with our hearts. It gave us time to better understand the importance of vulnerability in organizational leadership and among our peers. It helped us to learn repeatedly the reality that one doesn't make deals with God.

In the Hebrew Scripture, in Genesis 28, we read the intriguing story of Jacob and the ladder at Bethel, which descended at Bethel from heaven. God's promise to Jacob went something like this: "Jacob, I'm going to make you and your family and their descendants prosperous and numerous everywhere. And I'm going to make your family a blessing to everyone. And I'll always be with you."

Many reading this would probably utter a heartfelt "thank you" to the Lord for this promise and move on. But not Jacob. Jacob the dealer had to make a deal with God: "If you go with me and watch over me as I travel, and if you give me food and clothes and bring me safely home again, you will be my God." There was more to Jacob's deal, but you get the idea—"God, if you do this for me, then I'll do that for you."

Initially, that was the approach we wanted to take with God and my cancer. As leaders, though, the essence of our heart's debate with God ultimately took us in a different direction: the way of living with pain if necessary, and letting God be our sufficiency—indeed, letting God's grace be enough. God took us to the example of Job and reminded us of Job's words, "Though He slay me, yet will I trust in him."[32] He reminded us of the words in Daniel 3, by the three young men thrown into the fiery furnace: "We know, oh, King, that our God has the power to rescue us. But even if He doesn't we won't bow down to your God." I would have had much preferred Jacob's deal than the reality of the statement of the three about to be cast into the furnace. Gratefully, in my personal situation, the Lord healed.

Leaders who have found a way to engage their own hearts, as well as the hearts of those they lead, are more capable of understanding themselves and the persons they lead at higher and more authentic levels. The heart provides a window to the whole person and provides a level of authenticity and realness unknown to the head. Every person, including leaders and those within organizations, have been wounded in some way. They either have known or know pain, or arrows, as Eldredge calls them. When pain gets personal, it becomes one of life's best instructors in matters of the heart.

Further, personal pain teaches us more through "what" questions than "why" questions. According to Eldredge, a "why" question is the wrong question: "We're asking the wrong questions. Most of us are asking, 'God, why did you let this happen to me?' Or, 'God, why won't you just . . . (fill in the blank—help me succeed, get my kids to straighten out, fix my marriage)?'"

These and many other "why" questions are where all of us live. "Why" questions can also be victim or blame questions, often underlined with the assumption that someone else is to blame for my affliction or pain. Many of us have been there. Here is where contact with the heart can help, because, the heart can lead us to change the "why" questions to "what" questions: "[A] journey . . . with God requires a new set of questions [of God]. What are you trying to teach me here? What issues in my heart are you trying to raise through this? What is it you want me to see? What are you asking me to let go of?"[33] Fenelon adds to these points:

> See God's hand in the circumstances of your life. Do you want to experience true happiness? Submit yourself peacefully and simply to the will of God and bear your sufferings without struggle. Nothing so shortens and soothes your pain. . . .

(I)t will not stop you from bargaining with God. The hardest thing about suffering is not knowing how great it will be or how long it will last.[34]

Remember that God is not unaware of your suffering. He allows your suffering. See that He knows what is best for you. Live by faith as you embrace your trials. Confidently trust in God, even when you do not see what He is doing.[35]

Staying connected to the heart is what allows leaders to flourish as effective authentic leaders and to lead with integrity. This is why developing this soft skill is vital for effective leadership.

CHAPTER 5

Practice Consistent Fitness Renewal

"Take care of your body. It's the only place you have to live."[1]

—Jim Rohn

"Physical fitness is not only one of the most important keys to a healthy body, it is the basis of dynamic and creative intellectual activity."

—John F. Kennedy[2]

Fitness renewal is usually not the type of soft-skill competency that is regularly discussed at leadership conferences. It should be. There are usually dozens if not hundreds of topics presented during the usual three to four days of conference sessions. There are likely reasons for this absence, as there are some who likely don't see it as a priority or need. The reality is that fitness renewal—that is, getting in shape physically and sustaining fitness, holistically—is a soft skill that is indispensable for effective leadership.

Every year Marylou and I make our annual trek to the Mayo Clinic for our annual physicals. Mayo is an impressive place for all kinds of reasons. People are surprised, for example, to see the impressive collection of art displayed everywhere throughout the massive complex. There is, of course, the expected attention to holistic fitness renewal.

Displayed on one wall are posters that define Mayo's perspective on this, entitled "Twelve Habits of Highly Healthy People." There are the requisite foci on medical issues such as "preventive health care testing" and "address addictive behaviors." And there are the appropriate emphases on the need for good physical practices, such as physical activity; the need for strength and flexibility; getting adequate sleep; and making sure, in terms of diet, that appropriate attention is given to portion sizes eaten. These are all appropriate fitness renewal foci. But their focus on "healthy habits" also includes a more holistic emphasis.

Their remaining "habits" deal with one's emotional and spiritual health, focusing on the need to laugh, the importance of family and friends, the appropriateness of always practicing forgiveness and reflecting an attitude of gratitude, and the need to create space to quiet your mind. Finally, a remaining habit goes in the direction of creativity, to try something new. These habits, taken together, according to the Mayo Clinic, define the marks of highly healthy people.

People struggle in these fitness renewal areas, myself included. To the doubter, just wander around a meeting of CEOs sometime and observe. Not nearly enough participants are examples of fitness. My experience is one of sporadic fits and starts, of successes and failures, rather than the sustainable reality of fitness renewal that reflects an evenness and consistency of lifestyle. Because leaders are involved in lots of meetings, extensive travel, time away from home, and irregular eating hours, the task of fitness renewal remains demanding if not daunting. These reasons can become excuses, not justifiable reasons, for its absence.

Why Bother?

Marylou has an uncle who turned 104 in 2017. He lives in his own house, drives his own car, and prepares his own meals. He walks a mile every day and stays connected to family. We engaged him in conversation several months before he hit the century mark and asked

THE CHAPTER IDEA

Fitness renewal—especially fitness and diet—is essential to effective leadership. Taking action on the fitness renewal focus is often neglected because of other more pressing, more urgent issues. "Someday I'll get to take care of that issue."

Leaders need to wrestle to the ground their answer to the fitness renewal "Why bother?" question. Some leaders wait to give attention to fitness renewal until after the first heart attack, or until some other form of brokenness appears in their lives.

Leaders regularly confront the organizational issues they face at work. In the same way, they need to confront the care needed for themselves, so that they can continue to lead effectively.

Few leaders will face their maker with the lament, "I didn't spend enough time at the office." Boards need to ensure that fitness renewal appears at the top of the expectations they have for their chief executive, and for their senior leadership team

him to share with us keys to his longevity. He promptly answered, "That's the wrong question. The right question is 'why bother?'" Why bother getting up to exercise when you're tired? Why bother with taking the time to eat right? Why bother with getting involved in the community with others? Why bother with playing an instrument? He then went on to explain that there are immutable laws of nature that govern every part of life, and decisions or choices in this area also have consequences. He gave us this soft reminder that in this area of life, as in others, the question is, "So, what do you want? Why bother?" Why bother, indeed, is the question.

In the coming years there likely will be greater attention in appropriate ways to this matter of fitness renewal. There are multiple and increasing references to this subject, and almost all organizations are becoming increasingly concerned about the rising costs of health care. Questions are being raised about how employees who are unfit physically contribute to that increase in their health costs. Corporate wellness programs are showing dramatic increase. Part of the reason for this is the increasing activism and independence of shareholders and boards: "CEO health has gained greater attention in recent years. With boards increasingly independent and shareholders more vigilant, CEOs are more likely to be called on the carpet for any behavior considered unhealthy."[3]

Even voters and the news media have gotten into the act. Governor Chris Christie of New Jersey made national headlines for many months over his commitment, or the perceived lack thereof, to fitness renewal, with many questioning whether or not his weight issues would functionally prevent him from the stresses and demands of higher office.

All of us know we must constantly give attention to fitness renewal. This area provides an obvious opportunity where leaders need to set clearer boundaries and pursue improvement in managing margins. Some might question why it is included as a soft skill. The answer is simple. If hard skills are about what leaders do and soft skills are about how they go about doing what needs to be done, fitness renewal qualifies as a soft skill. It has everything to do with how leaders keep up their level of energy and the focus they need to bring to their leadership task.

This area is one of the key areas where I have struggled in the CEO leadership role. I have never found this to be an easy task. The older I get, the more intense the battle to practice fitness renewal. At any given time, I have used all of the excuses. Here's only a partial list:

- I'll get to it at a more convenient time.
- When I no longer have so many sit down meetings over meals, I'll eat better.
- I don't have the time to exercise (or, I'm too tired).
- The time zone change doesn't allow it.

There are many others. Nevertheless I refuse to fly the flag of surrender.

In the article, "Eight CEO Sacrifices,"[4] author Meryl Davids Landau notes fitness renewal as the number-three concern CEOs note as a downside to being a CEO. Search firm CEO Beverly Lieberman notes that "only half of the nation's top CEOs are exercising on a regular basis, although nearly all know they should. . . . They say they've got to do it, but most wait. Only after the heart attack do most find the time for it." Other health related issues derive from the "pressure of making key decisions, traveling through time zone changes, and not spending enough time unwinding."[5]

While not having had to face the reality of a heart attack, I have had to face the reality of cancer—an example of a Psalm 91 disease that strikes people in the dark. I don't know for certain when cancer came into my life, but part of it could have been a connection with the stress and busyness of my job, constant domestic and intense international travel, and lack of appropriate attention to a regular fitness regime.

Stress is often referenced as a burden of leadership, and because of its ubiquitous presence, we tend to ignore it. But stress simply *is*, and it has to be managed or it will manage and control leaders. A friend of ours recalls the following conversation with her doctor at the Mayo Clinic about the importance of stress management: "There's no such thing as 'just stress.' Stress causes or exacerbates most major illnesses. Your mind, body, and soul are connected. You are a package deal. . . . You can continue to take all those medications. Or you can do something that is harder, but in the long run,

better. You can go home and confront your life to see why you have
so much stress."[6]

The words "confront your life" represent the kind of self-discovery
referenced in an earlier chapter. But, in reality, the words "confront
your life" regarding fitness renewal are daunting reminders of a type
of self-discovery that is often left unexamined. Why is it often unexamined? Because in the lives of busy leaders, we often see this task as a
lower priority than the other more important ones. Even when we take
the time, we often ignore the results. We believe that there is a connection between how we engage in fitness renewal and our ability to
perform effectively as leaders, but we don't believe it enough to make
it happen. The leadership literature also reminds us of this connection.

From time to time the publication *Chief Executive* includes a
feature on an executive's favorite golf hole, implying support for
time away from the office on the golf course. Jeffrey Fox's perspectives about "How to Become CEO" represents another:

> Your brain will make you money, but your body carries
> your brain. The better your physical condition, the greater
> your capacity for productive, unrelenting work. And being in
> good physical condition gives you another edge. Ninety percent
> of all people climbing the corporate ladder are out of shape.
> You will be able to start earlier, pause less often and end your
> day with a wind sprint. You will also sleep better. You will be
> energetic and tire rarely. Your spirits will be up and you won't
> get depressed. . . . How you keep fit is up to you.[7]

There are cultural differences and geopolitical differences as to
how to address these needs. After I finished making a leadership development presentation to government leaders in East Africa, I asked a
senior official how life balance and fitness renewal is addressed and
embraced by his country's national leadership. The response was to

the effect that with so much work to be done and with people having so many needs, "we simply can't take the time to live that way. We take no time off, not even for vacations."

Yet, isn't that the paradox for leaders? We all know that without proper and regular attention to fitness, rest, and renewal we simply won't be able to handle the rigorous responsibilities required in leadership. Few leaders we know would be convicted of having spent too little time in the office and too much time in the fitness center. Sadly, the reality is often the opposite. For some reason, "the dinner-banquet-sample-the-pie-and-ice cream circuit" continues to frustrate and defeat. Marylou and I had one student campus event where we were asked to sample twenty-six groups of cupcakes as the way to select the winning cupcake team in a cupcake bake-off. To be sure we cut them into small sample bits, but still!

Often it is easier to criticize other "societal evils" than it is to focus on the damaging effects of limited exercise and poor eating habits. Oswald Sanders tells the story of Robert Murray McCheyne: "When . . . McCheyne was dying at the age of thirty-two—he had overspent himself in revival work and so forth—he told a friend at bedside, 'God gave me a horse to ride and a message to deliver. Alas. I have killed the horse and I can't deliver the message.'"[8] Sanders concludes, "I'm not suggesting for a moment that you become over solicitous for yourself or care for yourself too much or be afraid to spend. But there is a point when it is wise to stop and have a rest."[9]

Too many of us plead "guilty" to the charge leveled centuries ago by Fenelon: "You have abused your good health."[10] When we lived in New York City, I sometimes invited Dr. James Forbes, then the distinguished pastor at New York City's Riverside Church, to come and address our meetings. One time he spoke on this topic of fitness renewal, and I was impressed with his words: "The preacher's responsibility is to be as fit an instrument of the Holy Spirit as he or she can possibly be. We need to take care of ourselves emotionally, spiritually, and physically so that we can sustain our leadership capacity for our people."[11]

Fitness Renewal and Scripture

Some of the earliest references to fitness renewal come from the Scriptures. In particular, the Bible provides an overall framework and context for considering all kinds of fitness. Leviticus 23 is illustrative: "You have six days when you can do your work, but the seventh day of each week is holy, because it belongs to me. No matter where you live, you must rest on the Sabbath and come together for worship. This law will never change."[12] This text has relevance for leaders.

Living in New York City for fourteen years was an experience of a lifetime. We walked its streets, engaged in its hundreds of cultural offerings, and participated in the life of its churches. But unlike the 6/1 focus of Leviticus, New York City is dominated by a 24/7 mindset. Walk Times Square at midnight, for example, and you will see thousands of people on the sidewalk. To paraphrase the Frank Sinatra song, "If you can make it here, you can make it anywhere." So New Yorkers work more hours and are often handsomely rewarded for doing so, either financially or through the provision of perks—such as, in one industry, private car service to one's home in exchange for the late hours worked. We found it difficult to establish a regular routine within this 24/7 kind of lifestyle, so we built natural walking times rather than use of a taxi or subway as a way to compensate. True, our practically next-door New York Athletic Club provided tools for fitness in the form of a well-equipped facility, but international travel often hedged those opportunities. Rarely did our international travel carry-ons not include a pair of Rockport walking shoes.

So how should leaders grapple with these contemporary work realities? As a university president, I learned that walking the campus to meetings was far better than driving to meetings. Not only did walking provide more physical exercise, but it also provided countless additional opportunities for making contact with members of the broader university family. The number of opportunities discovered, the number of problems solved, and the number of relationships enhanced all dramatically increased simply through the habit of intentionally walking to meetings and events.

The emphasis of our Leviticus text gives guidance—rest, coming together, and worship. We believe all three have a role to play in providing a framework supportive of fitness renewal. The first emphasis includes the focus of stopping and stepping back from one's work. For leaders who love their work, stopping is just plain hard. Rest is difficult. Even on vacations, email is often being checked and phone calls are being made back to the office. Rest during vacation remains unprotected when full accessibility to the office is the dominant value. Regular cessation from work also provides the opportunity for fitness renewal to take place. If one is always working, rest simply won't happen. The text in Psalm 127:3 is very instructive: "It's useless to rise early and go to bed late, and work your worried fingers to the bone. Don't you know he [God] enjoys giving rest to those he loves?" Therefore, leaders are clearly called to make rest an integral part of a leadership lifestyle.

The second emphasis, to come together, again extends this cessation from work focus a bit further. When a person—leader or otherwise—together especially with friends, family, and loved ones steps away from work, there actually is relocation to some other place. The Scripture text seems to be saying that there is potential for renewal within a community. In community, others can encourage us, help carry our burdens, even exhort us. Yet, if we relocate, and take with us our phones, computers, and iPad, powered up and turned on, we've not really relocated anything except our hardware and devices, thus defeating the purpose for rest in the first place.

These, then, are two ways—rest and coming together—that we are given shelter from the 24/7 pressure of work. Importantly, we are encouraged to make space, yes, even at a fitness center, where we can focus on fitness renewal.

As has already been mentioned, the Leviticus text adds a third emphasis—we are called to worship—not just to rest and to come together. Here, clearly, we have in mind communities of worship that have as their focus worship of the transcendent God, as reflected in Psalm 29:2: "Honor the Lord for the glory of his name. Worship the Lord in the splendor of his holiness." This involves clearly setting our focus on another and away from ourselves.

Eugene Peterson notes that worship of something or someone other than ourselves runs counter to cultural thinking: "Our times are not propitious for worship. The times never are. The world is hostile to worship. . . . Some Christians get killed because they worship. . . . Worship shapes the human community in response to the living God. If worship is neglected or perverted, our communities fall into chaos or under tyranny."[13] If we neglect both personal and corporate worship, our lives and our leadership will likely experience the same end. By focusing on the transcendent God through worship, leaders are able to put their work and life issues in proper perspective, see their work or personal lives from a more important perspective, and in essence, experience another type of rest: rest for their souls.

The Proverbs state it this way: "The fear of human opinion disables; trusting in God protects you from that."[14] The words from 2 Corinthians 4 illustrate that kind of changed perspective that worship provides: "Even though on the outside it often looks like things are falling apart, on the inside, where God is making new life, not a day goes by without his unfolding grace. . . . There is more here than meets the eye. The things we see now are here today, gone tomorrow. But the things we can't see now will last forever."

Some folks reading this might summarily question the relevance of the Leviticus 23 passage to contemporary organizational life, arguing after all that "we're under grace, not law" and therefore Sabbath principles can be ignored. But that was certainly not Jesus' approach to the Sabbath, which He honored. These Sabbath principles point us in the direction of reclaiming the wisdom and balanced judgment of leaders past, yet equally needed by leaders present. For instance, in the Bible, Daniel was marked by his wisdom and balanced judgment, even in his selection of diet.[15]

Not Doing Everything That Needs to Be Done

Why do we in leadership have this overwhelming sense that we need to have a "doing more" orientation—raising more money, serving more people, and offering more programs? Do we delude ourselves into believing that if we just work long enough, hard enough, we'll eventually get caught up and then will be able to keep up with everything that the job calls us to do? Sometimes when I was asked before leaving the office if I had gotten caught up, my standard answer was, "No, I'm just stopping." In some cases, perhaps the overwork mode in which we engage is not about the job but rather about our need to demonstrate that we really belong, and that we're worthy of the positions in which we have been entrusted. In other words, our overwork is intended to prove something, to ourselves if not to others.

When we understand life through the eyes of a transcendent God; when we understand that the battles we fight are His, not ours; and when we come to the realization that as leaders we don't need to do everything that needs to be done, this frees us to place our focus where it needs to be, to align our priorities better with His—which ultimately provides the opportunity for us to live our priorities much better, including the time to pursue fitness renewal. We need to recognize anew that accomplishment, "even perfection, has its limits."[16] The words of Nancie Carmichael are helpful: "These days I believe we need to revisit the concept of keeping the

Sabbath. . . . the concept of taking time off to pace ourselves for our journey and to replenish us. As the angel told Elijah, 'Arise and eat; the journey is too great for you.'"[17]

Some are probably concerned with the statement that leaders don't need to do everything that needs to be done, that accomplishment has its limits. The thinking goes something like this: "Oh, yes, I do. My board fully expects me to carry out my job responsibilities." So we're up at the crack of dawn, pursuing long days and nights, often eating poorly, failing to exercise properly, and not stewarding well other important family priorities.

Yet here's the reality: Any leader can only do so much within his or her assigned leadership timeframe. We usually can't solve all the problems, build all the buildings, endow all the scholarships, serve everyone possibly needing or wanting to be served in the furtherance of the assigned mission.

Leaders give their best efforts to move the organization and its agenda forward on their watch, but then the leadership baton is— not *might be*, but *is*—handed to another, and the process is repeated, with the outgoing leader sometimes being soon forgotten. When leaders finally understand this reality, freedom is provided to do the right things, and there is freedom from not having to do everything that *could* to be done. This includes the focus on fitness renewal.

Interestingly, the Scriptures give strong support for learning leaders to pursue the kinds of things that are close to God's heart. Here's how I began to understand this better: Several years ago Marylou and I were reading the Scriptures. Our practice has been to read the Scripture texts in parallel and then discuss together what the Holy Spirit has taught through our separate readings. One day we focused on John 17:4: "I have brought glory to you here on earth by doing everything you gave me to do."

When we together started to reflect on this verse, I focused on "doing everything," and eagerly launched into my speech about needing to be better organized, more productive, and more effective so I could get more done. Frankly, my "to-do" list was already becoming unmanageable. Marylou patiently listened, then she quietly, but importantly, reminded me that I had missed one of the main teachings of the verse.

She focused on the words "you gave me to do." As she explained it, based on this verse and others, our priority work ought to be focused not on doing everything that could be done, but rather on what God has specifically given or called us to do. And that is the agenda that becomes our priority. Not my agenda, but His agenda. Jesus didn't do everything that could have been done. He didn't heal everyone who needed to be healed or give release to everyone in prison or provide food to everyone who was hungry. Yet He could truthfully say He had done "everything you gave me to do." And in that context, fitness renewal is something that God has called all of us to do as leaders. No excuses permitted.

Jesus is also an example of modeling fitness renewal as He regularly took time to rest.[18] One doesn't have to be in Israel very long to understand the reality, connected to both its geography and its topography, that walking hundreds of miles would have been a normative expectation for local citizens, including Jesus of Nazareth. Going back and forth between Capernaum and Jerusalem was not a short ten-mile walk on level terrain. Nevertheless, Jesus relentlessly focused on faithfully carrying out the work of His Father as He moved regularly from city to city, from area to area, doing nothing more, nothing less. He knew His Father's priorities for Himself, and so too must we.

Fenelon states our need to know God's priorities this way: "Everyone has his own work, but not everyone is doing the work which God has given him to do."[19] Fenelon challenged his readers to "take entire days just to withdraw and be alone with God. It is at the feet of Jesus that all the wounds of our heart are healed

and all of the soil of the world is wiped away."[20] He reminds us
to realize, "[Y]our busy life exhausts you in every way. Don't let
your work carry you away and eat up your life. Take time to renew
yourself before God. Be brief and act quickly with your business
affairs."[21] He adds:

> I will not think that you are growing spiritually until I see
> you have become calm enough to sleep peacefully without rest-
> lessness. . . . Live in peace. Your imagination is too active. It
> will eat you up! All that buzzing in your mind is like bees in a
> beehive. If you excite your thoughts, they will grow angry and
> sting you! How can you expect God to speak in His gentle and
> inward voice when you make so much noise? Be quiet and you
> will hear God speak. Live in the peace of Jesus.[22]

Is this not the place where we need to be as leaders as we continue the process of confronting our lives? Fitness renewal has a
place in this process. What truly should become the priorities for
us, our lives, and our families, whether at home or at work? If we
focus on what the Lord has given us to do, that focus will provide
a context and a direction—as well as a deterrent to our need to
believe we have to do everything that needs to be done.

In addition to the focus of the Hebrew Scriptures on Sabbath,
these scriptures also present a host of dietary laws for people to follow. Concerns about fitness renewal also appear in the apocryphal
book of Sirach: "A sound, healthy body and a cheerful attitude are
more valuable than gold or jewels. Nothing can make you richer or
give you greater happiness than these two things."[23]

In the writings of the New Testament, St. Paul has multiple references to fitness renewal, often using athletic or sports metaphors to
explain why we need to keep control over our bodies. He reminds
us of one of the primary reasons for this focus: "[Y]ou are God's

temple and that God's Spirit lives in you. . . . For God's temple is holy, and you yourselves are his temple."[24]

Again, one practical implication of this need to pursue fitness renewal is that we cannot be immersed in the work of the organization 24/7 and still attend to this important priority. There needs to be natural stopping points where time can be invested in priorities other than the workplace. When we take time—when we stop to invest in fitness renewal—it is not only an act of honoring the temple of God but also is an enhancement of practical and productive service in whatever calling God has placed on us.

The Struggle

One of the areas in which I struggle is getting away from my work. I may have physically relocated from the workplace, but mentally, I might still be fully engaged there. Once again, Fenelon speaks to this point:

> What you really need to do is sit quietly before God and your active and argumentative mind would soon be calmed.[25]
>
> Learn to listen to Him in silence so that you won't miss a word of what He says to you. You know a lot about outward silence, but little about inward silence. You must practice quieting your restless imagination. Stop listening to your unrenewed mind and the kind of logic it has. Get used to coming to God and asking Him for help when He asks you for something you are afraid to give.[26]
>
> Thinking too much will distract you. If you become trapped in your thoughts, they will blow out your inward spiritual sense like a wind blowing out a candle.[27]

Fenelon's struggle is often where I live. Sometimes I go on vacation, and it takes me days to pull away from my work. And by

PUTTING THE IDEA TO WORK

No matter how many times leaders have tried and perhaps failed at fitness renewal, there's always time to begin anew.

- Regarding the pervasiveness of the work agenda not allowing time for fitness renewal, the Scriptures provide a ready source of spiritual motivation, including references to honoring the Sabbath, and doing all things for the glory of God.
- Building and implementing an action plan with accountability—incorporating a work rhythm that includes work cessation, relocation, and worship—provides the systematic discipline that allows for both fitness renewal and the proper perspective about one's work.
- Leaders also need the discipline of setting proper life and work boundaries. Self-management is an important part of fitness renewal. Two simple daily

the time I have, I find myself preparing for reentry. My body may have gotten a rest, but my mind hasn't. As a result, we're trying to practice two approaches. On the one hand, we take longer but less frequent vacations; on the other, we take more frequent vacations of shorter duration. Marylou also reminds me that rather than working straight through the day, I need to take regular and practiced breaks, to provide mind rest that otherwise would not happen.

Looking at a city skyline, our visual image suggests the existence of buildings that are attached. But upon closer scrutiny, each of those buildings stands apart from the others, and each usually

> self-management disciplines are, where possible:
> —strive for achieving 9–10,000 steps or their
>   equivalent
> —record what is eaten
> Technology can easily record these accomplishments.
>
> Leaders who embrace fitness renewal are, in essence, saying yes to themselves. They understand fitness renewal as having a strong link to the achievement of their organizational agenda. They recognize the difference between doing everything there is to be done, and the freedom that comes from pursuing only those things *needing* to be done.
> To be sure, there is struggle involved in practicing these fitness renewal disciplines. But as long as this focus remains only an idea, not an action item, leaders are choosing, for them and for their families, to live the life of a gambler. Is that what they want?

has some kind of distinctive landscaping that sets it apart from the others and gives a visual break for the viewer. In seeing each building individually, we can enjoy its beauty and distinctive architecture. Short breaks taken between an unbroken string of appointments can have a similar effect on the mind and also on the persons we're meeting with. Clearing our minds refreshes our perspective and allows us to focus better on the next person or issue.

To summarize: The importance of fitness renewal is critical for effective leadership. This kind of renewal involves physical fitness to be sure, but as we have noted, it also involves the idea of Sabbath rest.

Rest, away from the 24/7 pressure of the workplace, is also an important focus and needs to include a focus on gathering for worship.

We have also highlighted the importance of understanding that there are limits to what any leader can accomplish. Accomplishment has limits. The focus needs to be on what God expects—and if the leader has a board, on what the board expects. This frees leaders from the pressure of feeling the need to do absolutely everything that needs to be done. At first this idea is frightening, especially for those driven types who are committed to doing everything they want to do. But once we understand the difference between the indiscriminate focus of trying to do everything versus the focus on doing only the priority things that need to be done, that understanding will provide a freedom for a more balanced life, and one more in keeping with God-ordained priorities. That is where we find the space to pursue fitness renewal.

Finally, I've avoided the temptation to provide a "how to" list for fitness renewal because this priority is already known. The key is to move this priority from idea to action. Many leaders eventually want to get to the implementation stage of fitness renewal—sometime, just not yet. But as long as it remains only an idea, and we keep putting off the decision to act, we are choosing to live the life of a gambler. Each person needs to approach fitness renewal with whatever plan works for them.

Two of the actions that work for me, particularly when it comes to eating the right things, is that I need to be accountable to myself on a daily basis. First, I try write down everything I eat, along with the number of calories connected to those eating choices. Second, I endeavor to get in at least ten thousand steps every day. Then I use an app on my smart phone that tracks both of these results. I'm convinced that just taking these two steps helps to make a positive difference.

We convince ourselves we'll get to that eventual point of necessary life change before we experience some adverse result of not doing so, like a broken marriage or family, or a heart attack. Some few may win that bet, but many others will lose it. The immutable laws of nature are a ticking time bomb that will catch up with us before we are ready. For some, "tomorrow" may never come.

The hope is that leaders will hear the question, "Why bother with fitness renewal?" and respond with eager action, fully embracing this soft skill as necessary and appropriate—now. Why? Because they know that if they do, they themselves, their families, and the organizations they lead will be better off because of it.

CHAPTER 6

Cultivate Creativity

"Every child is an artist until he's told he's not an artist."

—John Lennon[1]

"A true work of art is but a shadow of divine perfection."

—Michelangelo[2]

"There are flowers everywhere for those who want to see them."

—Henri Matisse[3]

"Every child is an artist. The problem is how to remain an artist once he grows up."

—Pablo Picasso[4]

We once lived in northwest New Jersey, near the Crayola Crayons factory store in Easton, PA. The brand name Crayola is one that most children, particularly in North America, grew up with. Who didn't have the ubiquitous box of multicolor Crayola crayons to use for coloring as a child? Being that this delightful factory store was nearby, Marylou once suggested we go on a "field trip" to Easton, to which I reluctantly agreed. I told myself that I was going to go to observe "the children." I would enjoy watching how crayons were made, learning just what activities they might have, and learn more about the world of color. I was anticipating a cognitive experience.

I went from section to section, floor to floor, watching and "enjoying" the various exhibits and demonstrations about how crayons were made, colored, packaged, and marketed. Fascinating. I'd make comments such as: "Our friends and their children would really enjoy this trip," and so on. Eventually, we got to a section that had crayons of every color imaginable, with delicious names like "blueberry pie" all amidst seemingly endless reams of "clean" blank paper. The message shouted to all who entered was this: "Explore, create and make something, using our crayons and other products." All around, people, mostly small children, were hard at work—using scissors, and all kinds of Crayola products. I was observing it all.

And then it happened. Marylou, herself an artist, went quickly to work. She hurriedly but beautifully sketched and colored, folded and cut, created and recreated. Then she looked over at me, and said something like, "Why are you just standing there watching and observing? Grab some paper, crayons, and start coloring something—anything—and don't be afraid to color outside the lines." My response? Sheer terror.

Discouraged as a Child

If I were five again, I would have responded to her invitation with joy and abandonment. I loved "coloring." I remember getting beautiful Crayola crayons as gifts, with dozens of beautiful colors nestled in straight rows and packed neatly together in the box. The bigger the box, the better. And color away I did, until one day in some school class, according to my teacher, my coloring became no longer adequate. I was told I had no artistic talent. So, when the art competitions came along, I simply slinked back to the corner, deferring to others. My interest in art was put on hold.

The same thing happened with music. I grew up in a home where we did a lot of singing, mostly hymns. Classical music was absent. I knew little about Bach, Brahms, Beethoven or other famous composers. When I first was introduced to classical music, I shifted my interest from guitar and drums to violins and trumpets. I loved the sound of them all. I thought it must be what heaven might sound like. I was eagerly looking forward to learning more about classical music in my junior high "fine arts" class. The teacher introduced us to all kinds of wonderful composers and artists. Then one day we were asked to write down our "feelings" and "impressions" about what we had just heard and experienced. I wrote feverishly and effortlessly. Sadly, to me at least, was the teacher's total rejection of what I had written. He called it "sheer nonsense," and his comment at that moment totally eviscerated whatever interest I then might have had in classical music. I turned to other interests, especially sports. My interests in classical music were also put on hold.

My junior high teacher's response to how I interpreted the music I heard decades earlier reminded me of an Eric Metaxas comment in his masterpiece, *Bonhoeffer: Pastor, Martyr, Prophet, Spy.* Writing about young Dietrich's first trip to see the masterpieces in Rome, he records Bonhoeffer's frustration about the interpretations being given by the then-current art historians: "[T]he current art historians are the worst guides. Even the better ones are awful. . . . There is no criterion for their interpretation and its correctness. . . . Yet our whole thinking process is regulated by it. . . . When one doesn't have to interpret, one should just leave it alone. . . . A work of art [or music—my addition] viewed with clear intellect and comprehension has its own effect on the unconscious."[5]

That is exactly what I had felt about how others had reacted to my responses to art and music. Decades later I echo Bonhoeffer's frustration: "[W]hen one doesn't have to interpret, one should just leave it alone." As one scarred artistically in the early years of my life, I had to rebuild and nourish my interest in the arts, now such a blessing.

Therefore, being told to "color outside the lines" decades later simply terrified me. By that time I had completed three graduate degrees, including a law degree and a PhD from reputable universities. I had spent much time in intellectual discovery and theoretical analytics. I had already completed one ten-year university presidency and was then serving as president of another leading New York based non-profit. Now here I was at the Crayola factory, immobilized by the words "color outside the lines." Why?

Academic Training Didn't Do It

All of my academic training taught me many things, but creativity and doing art were not on the list. My CEO leadership experiences had taught me to stay within the lines, whether adherence to a strategic plan once developed, budget parameters once approved, board policy once implemented, or alignment with the mission once established. The key to good budget control is to stay within the lines. In other words, to ask me or other students of leadership to color outside the lines goes against almost everything we have experienced or been taught as leaders. The inference was that the really good leaders focus on the "hard" stuff, things such as managing budgets, pursuing conservative financial analysis, exploring the particulars of market research, not taking undue risks, and staying "up-to-date" with technology strategy.

Julia Cameron, in her classic *The Artist's Way Workbook*, encourages people like me to face this question: When did staying within the lines become the norm? She notes:

> [Y]ou do not need to know why something works in order to have it work. As a rule, too much thinking is a part of being blocked. Artists and intellectuals are not the same animal.

This causes a great deal of confusion. Our schools educate us intellectually but not artistically. We learn how to deconstruct art, not construct it. . . . Our mythology around art is very damaging. Our culture teaches us that creativity is a frightening pursuit. . . . We are far more creative than we imagine.[6]

In essence, Cameron is suggesting that we cannot *think* our way to creativity as much as we *do* our way to creativity: "[W]e awaken our creativity by using it, not through theory. You will not learn to be fearless, but you will learn how to create despite your fears."[7]

Several years ago I was attending a conference of university presidents. The overall theme was dealing with presidential leadership in tough times. We all knew that indeed the times were tough, perhaps tougher than at any other time in the history of higher education. Each of us recognized that maybe we were currently seeing only the tips of the icebergs that we would face in the years ahead.

One of our plenary speakers was the president of the Art Institute of Chicago, Dr. Walter Massey. After discussing the many challenges faced by the contemporary leader, he offered "key drivers" to help manage and lead during turbulent times. I eagerly embraced and acknowledged each one of his points:

> 1) the importance of vision and mission ("nothing new here," I quickly concluded);
> 2) enhancing quality ("of course, that's a no-brainer");
> 3) institutional loyalty ("again, of course");
> 4) organizational effectiveness ("yawn"); and
> 5) creativity ("yikes!").

He went on to explain that as leaders we all need to be "explorers," noting that playful creativity is essential to social and economic entrepreneurialism.

What is playful creativity? Leaders have often heard of the need to create new businesses, new jobs, new programs, and new solutions to meet new needs—in essence, to think outside the box. The leadership mantra of the moment is, "We'll not be able to 'cut the budget' enough to manage our way out of our financial distress." And all of us have heard the saying: "If you always do what you've always done, you'll always get what you've always got. Now is that what you want?" But here was a distinguished former liberal arts university president—now art institute president—linking effective leadership to creativity and artistic expression, and identifying the need for creativity as a distinctive leadership soft skill. Indeed, he was challenging all of us as college and university presidents to engage in more personal creativity and to foster more creativity in the workplace. I was reminded of the late Peter Drucker's challenge to business schools to focus more on opportunity finding, not just on problem-solving.

Then a light bulb went on about my Crayola "outside the lines" experience of many years before. At some time in my life I had pushed down the creative, artistic side of me. I had subordinated the "soft" stuff, to the "hard" stuff, in essence, the analytical, intellectual side of me. At some time in my life, I had concluded that only the "hard" skills mattered in management and leadership, and if "soft" skills were in play, they were far less relevant and certainly less important. Coloring outside the lines at its worst was a frightening, unpredictable experience.

Or, at its best, could it become an act of faith? Again, to paraphrase Cameron, art is a spiritual act. It takes faith to move onto the page, the stage, the easel—or the leadership platform of leading in uncharted waters.

I was not alone as a leader as someone not gifted in coloring outside the lines, as I have heard this from many other leaders. In the words of another, I had to come face to face with this question: "If you want your team members to think outside the box, why are you coloring inside the lines?"[8] Here I was learning from Dr. Massey that leaders without an authentic creative side may ultimately be unprepared, if not inadequate, for the contemporary demands of leadership. Why? Because of our inability to color outside the lines, or to think outside of the proverbial box, we may be unable to see, let alone understand, the multifold new opportunities that are everywhere, all around us.

Creativity Is Essential to Effective Leadership

The Economist made this point in an interesting way. In an article titled "The Art of Management,"[9] this bifurcation of the differences between art and business is stated clearly:

> "Artists routinely deride business people as money-obsessed bores. . . . Many businesspeople, for their part, assume that artists are a bunch of pretentious wastrels. Bosses may stick a few modernist daubs on their boardroom walls. They may go on corporate jollies to the opera. They may even write the odd cheque to support their wives' bearded friends. But they seldom take the arts seriously as a source of inspiration."

The article also notes that "the bias starts at business school, where 'hard' things such as numbers and case studies rule. It is reinforced by everyday experience. Bosses constantly remind their underlings that if you can't count, it doesn't count. Quarterly results impress the stock market; little else does." Simply put, "business people nevertheless have a lot to learn by taking the arts more seriously." The article then listed several ways business leaders can learn from the arts:

> 1) Many artists are also superb entrepreneurs;
> 2) "[S]tudying the arts can help businesspeople communicate more effectively-many of the world's most successful businesses are triumphs of story-telling more than anything else";

> ## THE CHAPTER IDEA
>
> Creativity is a soft skill that celebrates outside-the-box thinking, and can catalyze innovation and change.
>
> The difficulty is that many leaders, for a variety of reasons, have either shunned or stifled their creative instincts, choosing to live life without coloring outside the lines, both personally and organizationally.
>
> Other leaders separate their creative "artsy" life from their organizational responsibilities, because they fail to see the connection between creativity and effective organizational leadership. They settle instead for art as decoration, hanging beautiful pieces around the office complex rather than getting themselves directly involved with creativity.
>
> Leaders who cultivate organizational creativity seek to embed this focus, both in the culture where they serve and in the people they lead.

3) "Studying the arts can also help companies learn how to manage bright people. . . . [T]oday's most productive companies are dominated by . . . 'clevers,' who are the devil to manage. They hate being told what to do by managers, whom they regard as dullards. They refuse to submit to performance reviews. In short they are prima donnas. The arts world has centuries of experience managing such difficult people"; and

4) "Studying the art world might hold out the biggest prize of all—helping business become more innovative." [10]

A *Fast Company* interview between then-Disney Television president Anne Sweeney and British educational theorist Ken Robinson focused on the relationship and linkage between art, creativity, and the business world: "[A]ctually companies need people who can think differently and adapt and be creative. . . . Imagination [is] the most extraordinary set of powers that we take for granted: the ability to bring into mind the things that are not present." Then Sweeney discussed how, in doing portraiture art, she sometimes has to deconstruct a painting to get a better perspective on what she's trying to accomplish: "And in some ways, [deconstructing faces and putting them back together], that has helped me at work in deconstructing problems: looking at them from different angles."[11]

So we come full-circle. Leaders know of the need for creativity and innovation throughout their organizations and spend lots of time talking about it. Everyone these days talks about the importance of catalyzing entrepreneurs. Yet paradoxically, much leadership learning falls short in these important areas, focusing more heavily instead on the hard, measurable, conceptual, analytical realities of organization. Are these realities irrelevant and unimportant and unnecessary to organizational life? Clearly not. But are they enough, are they sufficient to help lead us into a more entrepreneurial and innovative future? Probably not.

Fast Company continues to be one of the contemporary business magazines that regularly discusses these softer business and management realities, including the concept of business design. Its article "Generation Flux" noted the transitory reality of the business world. Companies that were exalted and held up as market leaders relatively recently are now struggling for relevance, if not survival. What happened? Did they lose their ability to manage the budget? Were their financial analytics faulty? The reality is that companies like Nokia and Motorola lost out to the improved creativity and design embraced by companies such as Apple and Samsung.

How, then, might a leader embrace creativity? Here are some suggestions.

PUTTING THE IDEA TO WORK

Leaders need to understand and celebrate the diversity of creativity in all of its forms, not just in the typical but important areas of art and music.

- It is better to nurture this focus organizationally than to mandate it. Leaders need to create space and time in which creativity can happen.
- Leaders themselves need to practice and model their commitment to creativity, perhaps choosing to engage personally in some creative, artistic endeavor.
- Leaders who embrace creativity intentionally surround themselves with creative people.

Leaders who champion creativity within the organization make it a systemic focus rather than settle for something like a department of creativity. Creativity must, in some way, become a part of everyone's organizational focus.

Some Creativity Techniques

First, leaders understand that creativity comes in different formats and reflects different gifts. It doesn't always look the same for everyone. The person who can envision or imagine an unseen new product or building might not be able to do anything with a painter's easel. The person who can create a sonata might be a lousy singer. The person who can copyright an idea or trademark a book or patent an invention might be a poor designer. We need to celebrate differences, in both creative expression and design.

Second, leaders understand that creativity can't be mandated. According to Ken Robinson, "creative thinking doesn't happen by forcing it." But perhaps leaders can nurture creativity by modeling it. There is a process to creativity that happens, where "your mind doesn't turn off. . . . I keep a pad of paper and pen by me at night, because things just occur to you."[12] As Todd Henry puts it in *The Accidental Creative*, "To unleash your creative potential now and thrive over the long term, you need to establish your own rhythm, one that is independent of the expectations and pressures you face each day."[13] In essence, leaders need to create space to allow creativity to thrive.

Third, leaders personally continue to learn and practice creativity in new ways. They recognize the importance of both establishing and modeling a culture that celebrates creativity. Leaders push themselves to learn and perhaps become artists in new ways as they, too, model the creativity expected of others. A leader ought to practice creativity in some way. As Sweeney puts it, "I manage, based on the very simple belief that adults continue to learn. Too many times adults walk into situations and people have already been put into a box." That is, the assumption is made that they have stopped learning. They should push back on that assumption and personally model it.

Sweeney's point requires further discussion. People make efforts at some stage of their lives to figure themselves out and then simply lock it in. Conclusions are drawn, often erroneously, that push people in one direction or another—"I am not good at art or music"— and then we lock in that conclusion. We freeze. To Sweeney's point, I either put myself in a box or I allowed others to put me there.

Why do we choose to stop learning when it comes to creativity in any area, including the arts? More specifically, why did I, in my youth, hand over the keys to someone else in this one very important aspect of my life? And why is it still being done by so many? Often, our excuse is that it's not in our nature to be creative. Then why don't we allow ourselves to be nurtured in these areas, rather than just remaining in our noncreative boxes labeled "do not disturb"? The key question is not how have we been gifted by nature or gifted by the nurture of someone else in these important areas. The key question is, now knowing of its essential importance in leadership, how will I continue to pursue this personally and in my leadership? This is the challenge I have for myself, and this is the challenge we all need to champion as leaders.

Interestingly, leaders often emphasize the importance of leadership development for their staffs but unfortunately fail to model it—in effect, undercutting the very message they're trying to send to others. Often the older a leader becomes, or, the more entrenched a leader becomes in a leadership role, the more difficult it sometimes becomes to keep learning.[14] Effective leaders personally embrace the reality that the future belongs to the learning, not to the learned—especially so in this area of creativity and the arts.

One of the very helpful creative processes I learned about in my last presidency was the use of the "charette" process as a way to think about designing new facilities. A charette is "a meeting in which all stakeholders in a project attempt to resolve conflicts and map solutions."[15] Done in different ways, the way we approached our charette at Taylor was to first ask university program staff to work hard at defining the program that a new facility will house. Then we invited three different architect firms to come to campus, work on shared teams with our staff, and thereafter design multiple creative options capable of housing the intended program. We found that the charette process generated far more creativity than if we had worked with only one firm. As a result of embracing this process, the architectural firm eventually selected was one from those firms participating in the initial charette process. The charette process would work equally well with program design.

Fourth, leaders intentionally hire and surround themselves with others who are creative in ways different from themselves. They seek to create a balance of giftings at the leadership table. Sometimes potential candidates for positions are marginalized because they are creative types rather than analytical types. It is important that leaders ensure that creative types have a place at the table. Leaders understand that failure to invest in creative thinking and creative people will likely limit the kind of outside-of-the-box type of thinking and organizational advantage that may ultimately lead to organizational reinvention, if not to organizational salvation. Clearly creativity is an effective soft skill that is necessary for organizational flourishing. Leaders will ensure that creative types are embedded in appropriate ways within the core power places of their organizations.

Fifth, leaders understand that there is an important link between creativity and teamwork. The creative act usually doesn't take place in isolation from others but rather in the presence of others. The creative act requires listening to others, observing others, and learning from others. All of that input, coupled with the "being" part of the one who creates, contributes to the result. Madeleine L'Engle says it this way: "When I am constantly running, there is no time for being. When there is no time for being, there is no time for listening. . . . Our story is never written in isolation. We do not act in a one-man play. We can do nothing that does not affect other people, no matter how boldly we say, 'It's my own business.'"[16]

As the *Fast Company* focus in "Generation Flux" illustrates, the days of distress and difficulty in many ways are just the beginning of what will likely characterize organizational life for the foreseeable future. In the college and university world, the book *College (Un) Bound* identifies multiple ways that outside-the-box thinking has begun to change that world. It notes that for those organizations that survive, it will likely be because they understand the importance of creativity, driven by outside-the-box thinking.[17]

Thus far in this discussion, we have focused primarily on the organizational side of leadership, stressing the importance of the soft skill of creativity to organizational health and effectiveness. The temptation of the leader might be something like this: "Okay, so we'll hire more artistic, more creative types" and leave it at that. I want to argue, however, that to look at creativity as perhaps only a department—as a place where someone else does creative things, rather than as something that everyone in the organization must champion—is to remain as I did at the Crayola factory. I was happy to have someone else color outside the lines, but not me. But creativity is personal, and every leader needs to develop his or her creative side, whatever that looks like.

L'Engle, in her book *Walking on Water*, adds to this thought. She observes that creativity is personal, and involves every person: "But unless we are creators, we are not fully alive. . . . Creativity is a way of living, no matter our vocation or how we earn our living."[18] In essence, she argues that creativity must be personal, and not limited only to a few artist types or an organizational perspective: "Creativity is not limited to the arts."[19] Everybody has creative potential waiting to be unleashed.

L'Engle describes the unleashing of this personal creative potential like this: "The artist is a servant who is willing to be a birth giver. . . . Each work of art, whether it is a work of great genius, or something small, comes to the artist and says, Here I am. Enflesh me. Give birth to me. The artist either says yes—'my soul doth magnify the Lord'—or refuses. Not everyone has the humble courageous obedience of Mary."[20]

To summarize: Each person in organizational leadership has a responsibility to personally pursue his or her creative potential and creative giftedness. Sometimes that personal creativity is deferred until after retirement, when persons then take up writing, art, music, or gardening. But why wait? Why not begin now? Don't wait until retirement. The times urgently cry out for creative, entrepreneurial leadership. There are multifold opportunities still waiting to be identified and explored, certainly in our organization and perhaps yours. A leader's creativity, however expressed, will make him or her more effective and the organizations they serve more productive. As Anne

Sweeney notes, "Art has been good for my soul."[15]

So what are you waiting for? "Color away, and don't be afraid to go outside the lines." Both you and the organization you serve will be better for it.

CHAPTER 7

Enhance Trust

"We're never so vulnerable than when we trust someone—but paradoxically, if we cannot trust, neither can we find love or joy."

—Walter Anderson[1]

"He who does not trust enough, will not be trusted."

—Lao Tzu[2]

"Most good relationships are built on mutual trust and respect."

—Mona Sutphen[3]

◆ One of the most important realities of soft skill leadership is the need to understand the importance of trust, especially in organizational life. Most of us can remember hearing the word from our parents, in words such as "just trust me." What does that mean? Trust is seldom defined. The assumption is that almost everyone knows what it is. When it is absent, the person who is not trusted experiences severe pain.

Stephen Covey says it this way: "Trust is the one thing that is common to every individual, relationship, team, family, organization . . . which if removed, will destroy the most powerful government, the most successful business . . . the most reflective leadership, the greatest friendship, the strongest character, the deepest love. . . . That one thing is trust."[4]

I was standing in front of a group at the university, listening to a string of successive speakers identify the multiple ways I had failed to deliver the right perspective or the right solution for the university regarding particular issues. The pain I felt from each speaker seemed to intensify. Some had shared their comments with me in advance so I knew what they were going to say. My overall reaction, having heard from all of them, was that I was no longer worthy of being trusted, and that I no longer deserved to lead. As it turned out, my reaction was misplaced; nevertheless, the initial perceived absence of trust was devastating.

Trust Defined

According to dictionary.com, trust involves the idea of "the integrity, strength, ability . . . of a person or thing; confidence." Webster.com notes that trust is a "belief that someone or something is reliable, good, honest, effective . . . an assured reliance on the character, ability, strength, or truth of someone or something."[5]

Probably one of my favorite definitions of trust comes from Covey, who defines trust this way: "Simply put, trust means confidence. The opposite of trust—distrust—is suspicion."[6] Elsewhere, he says, "Trust is a function of both character (which includes integrity) and competence."[7] Trust is the gift given to those in authority, that the best interests of those not present in the room will be attended by those who are: "When I trust someone, I am saying that in matters affecting my welfare, I believe that the one trusted will be concerned about me and will diligently work for the betterment of my interests."[8] This is the idea expressed by John Gardner: "A loyal constituency is won when people, consciously, judge the leader to be capable of solving their problems and meeting their needs."[9] Covey again adds, "No wonder that the argument is made

THE CHAPTER IDEA

Without question, trust is the glue that holds organizations together.

Trust is like a bridge that has to be carefully built, with a solid foundation people can cross and use for other purposes. Effective leaders make developing and enhancing trust a top organizational priority.

When trust deteriorates, regardless of the reason, the ability of an organization to effectively function is severely damaged, if not destroyed.

A foundation for trust can be found in many places in the Scriptures—"Love . . . always trusts," for example (1 Cor. 13:6–7). We live our lives based on the belief that God is trustworthy. He can be trusted. So, too, must we.

In organizational life, mutual trust is what allows effective work to be completed. Trust can't be bought or transferred; it must be earned. When trust no longer exists, leadership change is often the result.

Because of the complexity of organizations, the ability to trust sometimes looks different within various constituencies, as these different constituencies often have conflicting desires or needs.

that trust . . . is the key leadership competency of the new global economy."[10] No wonder I have identified focusing on trust as an essential soft skill.

Getting trust right is critically important for leaders. All constituencies in a healthy organization need to have a mutual respect and trust for each other. As Gardner notes, "There is much to be gained for any leader in winning the trust of constituents. . . . Leaders must not only forge bonds of trust between themselves and their constituents, they must create a climate of trust throughout the system over which they preside. Trust is not the only glue that holds a human group together, but when it dissolves, the capacity of the group to function effectively is seriously impaired."[11]

A Biblical Framework

For those who embrace the teachings of the Bible, we are challenged to trust God. One reference, and there are many that illustrate how and who we must trust, is found in Proverbs 3:5–6: "Trust in the Lord with all your heart; do not depend on your own understanding. Seek his will in all you do, and he will show you which path to take." Another is found in Psalm 37:5: "Commit everything you do to the Lord. Trust him, and he will help you."Earlier in my life, I remember singing hymns in church, such as, "Tis so sweet to trust in Jesus / Just to take Him at His word," which I sometimes struggled to do. The words of these hymns were in essence calls to trust God, and they called for a response, such as "Jesus, Jesus, how I trust Him" and "Trust and obey / there's no other way."

Clearly, these Scriptures and their musical progeny are calls for us to trust in the vertical sense. We are called to trust God with our lives. The Scriptures call us to trust each other in the horizontal context as well. Part of how we learn to trust each other, though, relates in part to the assumptions we make about each other, and the attitudes we have about others, whether at home or in the workspace.

Paul the apostle clearly set forth the mutual standards we are to aspire to. For example, note Philippians 4:8 (CEV): "Finally, my friends, keep your minds on whatever is true, pure, right, holy, friendly, and proper. Don't ever stop thinking about what is truly worthwhile and worthy of praise." This exhortation is directly applicable to how we should approach relationships with each other, regardless of position or role, whether at work or at home.

Paul affirms this approach by clearly stating similar expectations in relationships by talking about what love is in 1 Corinthians 13, especially verses four through seven: "Love is patient, love is kind. It does not envy, it does not boast, it is not proud. It is not rude, it is not self-seeking, it is not easily angered, it keeps no record of wrongs. Love does not delight in evil but rejoices with the truth. It always protects, always trusts, always hopes, always perseveres."

Are these words—especially the Scriptures—just ink and paper, to be forgotten when the determination is made that God or people are no longer trustworthy? Can we simply dismiss these words when we go to work for an organization, somehow subsuming these truths instead in favor of the pervasiveness of longstanding community culture? Or are these words bedrock realities that inform our ability or inability to trust in any context, including organizational context?

These words seemingly have broad application to every person, every position, in every setting. Regarding this matter of trust, the Bible is clear: "Love always trusts," at both the horizontal and vertical levels. So perhaps, just perhaps, when people within an organization stop trusting each other, it may be indicative of other concerns, other issues. Something else may be going on.

Interestingly, the words of Scripture regarding the need for people always to trust, and to focus on the praiseworthy elements of the other, seem to align with others' observations about the workplace. For instance, writing in the *HBR Blog Network*, Robert Pozen discussed "The Delicate Art of Giving Feedback."[12] He observed that not only do people respond more strongly to negative feedback (five times more strongly in marriage, and six times more strongly in the workplace), they also respond generously to praise. In "The Ideal Praise-to-Criticism Ratio" Jack Zenger and Joseph Folkman observe that unless an enterprise is headed "over the cliff," the praise-to-criticism ratio . . . needs to "endeavor to move the proportion closer to the ideal of 5.6

to 1."[13] What does trust look like in organizational life? Are there types of trust and different ways trust is practiced? How might trust be strengthened within organizations, and within the multiple and sometimes competing constituencies that mark organizational life?

Mutual Trust Is Foundational

In the personal and organizational sense, trust needs to be both foundational and mutual. Leaders may be concerned about whether or not people trust them. At the same time, these people are wondering whether or not they are trusted by their leaders. Without a shared sense of mutuality and commitment, the personal and organizational space where trust resides will be totally empty. Unfortunately, that is often the reality.

Because of the limitations of the human condition, trust is not our natural bent. There will always be occasions not to trust. While the desire of my heart may be to trust without limitation, the practical realities are often considerably different. We ought not to confuse, however, the difficulty of achieving mutual trust with the assumption that it is simply impossible to achieve. We have to be careful to avoid confusing difficulty with impossibility.

Trust is an essential ingredient—maybe the most essential ingredient, almost like food and water—for all of organizational life at both the vertical and horizontal levels. When people know they are trusted, they are empowered. And when they're not, disempowerment follows. Trust is the glue that binds and helps establish and maintain relationships, and helps keep organizations and families together and focused.

Take marriage, for example. What hope is there in the marriage where a couple doesn't trust each other, where suspicion reigns and cynicism abounds? Or for a family, when neither the parents nor the children trust each other? Dysfunction rules, and chaos is the result. But so, too, for organizations. Trust seems to be the cement that helps hold things together. Mutual trust appears to be the foundation that enables people and organizations to get through their difficult seasons, ultimately enabling both to flourish.

Trust is not something that can be endowed, or bought or sold on the open market. At the risk of being simplistic, one can't go into the convenience market and buy two packages of trust. Trust can't be demanded or insisted upon through the use of position or power, nor can it be established by a resolution by a board. How does a leader obtain trust? Trust must be earned; it must be nourished, and again, ideally, it should be mutual. Not only should the people believe in their leaders, but the leaders should also believe the people entrusted to their leadership and care.

Trust in Perspective

I believe that trust is contextual—that is, it is influenced by what has previously transpired in the life of the one being asked to trust. If people have had positive experiences in childhood or in a previous work environment, the presumption in favor of trusting is brought with them to the workplace. Of course, the opposite is also true: One who has experienced distrust brings the bias against trusting someone else into their lives, and accordingly, into the workplace and at home. In the workplace, and based on prior experiences, people may be biased or predisposed to trust in a particular direction, positively or negatively.

This also applies to leaders. If leaders have had negative experiences with trust in former leadership assignments or in personal situations, that context also affects their ability to trust. Manfred F.R. Kets de Vries[14] details the various ways leaders with dysfunctional pathologies can hobble an organization. Though he doesn't reference the toxicity of a prior failed trust as adversely impacting an organization, I have certainly seen those results. Again, context may color one's ability to trust and to be trusted.

An organization's history can either positively or negatively provide a context that enhances trust or distracts from it. It is not unusual to hear the stories of a failed trust that ultimately became an integral part of the organizational legacy. People remember promises made but not kept. When there is a succession of broken promises, people become inoculated against trusting in the future. When trust is a healthy part of an organization, the opposite happens—and mutual trust is the result. Successive examples of mutual trust provide building blocks that strengthen positive trust. Again, personal and organizational experiences will adversely or positively impact what happens next with regard to organizational trust.

Differentiated Trust

In addition to the importance of context, trust needs to be differentiated. There may be different levels of trust within an organization at the same time, and within differing organizational constituencies. For example, within a university community four of the primary constituencies are the board of trustees, the faculty, the student body, and the staff. Because of the nature of the university mission, the faculty is given an important chair within the internal university constituency orchestra. So, too, the board—the legal owner of the university.

There also can be differing levels of trust within these four groups with regard to the organization's leader. One group might have low trust for the leader, while another group can have high trust. When other external constituencies are added (groups such as donors, alumni, parents, and the local community), there could be considerable trust differentials within those groups as well. As a result, trust within an organization gets complicated. That is why sometimes boards of trustees are often strongly supporting their president at the very same time a faculty might be voting "no confidence" in the same person—a reality often reported in higher-education news media.

The reason for mentioning this idea of differentiated trust is to caution leaders to avoid succumbing to the human desire to simply average trust across all constituent groups. For example, if the faculty gives me a C in trust, and the board gives me an A, I should be careful not to conclude that my overall trust score is a B. Leaders should not conclude that because there is high trust in certain constituencies, they can ignore low trust in others. That would be a mistake.

Trust should not be viewed as a generic reality across the organization. Rather, leaders need to understand where each of the groups within the organization are at, with regard to trusting each other and leadership, in order to know how and where to address appropriate lack-of-trust concerns. This, in part, is what I believe the Bible is saying when it challenges shepherd-leaders to "know well the conditions of their flocks," a teaching referenced in Proverbs 27:23. Interestingly, enhancing trust across all constituencies is marked with consistent practices and behaviors. Solid behaviors that help enhance and build damaged trust are the very same behaviors that keep trust strong within all constituencies.

Actions Which Trigger Distrust

Just as trust has a context, and just as trust may be differentiated, there are also certain issues or actions within organizations that may inherently trigger distrust or at least severely impair the ability to trust. Clearly, those issues often revolve around difficulties connected to budget and compensation. There are of course, other triggers, but these two are regularly referenced when trust is lacking. Overall organizational budgets that support flourishing mission accomplishment as well as provide more-than-adequate compensation adjustments serve as shock absorbers that protect organizational trust when there are other difficulties. But take those shock absorbers away and trust concerns become exacerbated. Here are a couple of examples.

At two of the organizations where I have served, we have had to engage in dramatic personnel reductions. At one place, we had to reduce staff by around twenty-five percent. At another, I ended up recommending the closure of a campus, with only a relative handful of persons retaining employment. Both actions were triggered by future mission and financial viability concerns. So the question to be raised is this: How can trust be regained in these kinds of situations?

Having lived those realities several times over, is it naïve to believe that high trust can be maintained in the midst of these kinds of situations? In my thirty-five years as a president, I've seen very few people who have evidenced high levels of trust after being told that their employment has ended. Losing a job is traumatic, and goes to the heart and soul and economic stability of a person's life. Decisions that ultimately result in job loss are among the most difficult to make, if not the most difficult, across a wide range of executive decisions. So, are decisions that result in potential job loss harbingers of the ultimate loss of organizational trust? Maybe. Maybe not. It all depends. But often those types of decisions have to be made in order to ensure mission viability and to save the positions of many others.

Every leader is regularly making deposits into his or her organizational "you can trust me" account. These deposits are ongoing, consistent, connected to repeated dependable behaviors, and come from consistent actions that say to people: "You are cared for at this place. We hear you." Alternately, leaders know that there will be situations that test organizational trust, that put trust at risk. The hope is that the leader's trust account will be robust enough to sustain trust hits—not if they come but when they come, especially regarding those decisions that involve personnel reductions or major budget realignments.

In the same way, effective leaders understand the reality of "achievable trust"—that is, they seek the highest level of trust possible in a given situation, no matter the difficulty. They understand that "perfect" trust, or the highest possible level of trust, is often unachievable in certain circumstances. In the area of private higher education, for instance, the media are often filled with stories of cutbacks and personnel downsizings. As already mentioned, these kinds of decisions, no matter how cleverly communicated, are not trust-enhancers. It is important to focus instead on what levels of trust might be achievable when those decisions appear to be inevitable.

When the very difficult decision was made to close a campus, it was important for me to ensure that the commitments I made during that time of crisis were fully honored and carried out after the crisis passed. Those promises are remembered. The promises I made needed to result in an action reflective of those promises. I have been encouraged to hear from multiple sources, "You have kept your word." As we took steps to fulfill those promises, it has been encouraging to hear years later about how God had remained faithful to those impacted during those difficult days.

Someone has said that when it comes to keeping promises, "It is time to stop talking, to start walking, and to let our feet catch up with our mouths." It is also important for those not affected in a crisis of trust to have the sense that others impacted by such an event were treated honorably, and that the processes used to achieve the end results were fully appropriate. As Covey notes, "It's not just how we behave that affects trust. It's also the interpretations people make of those behaviors and the conclusions drawn from them that affect trust."[15]

In times of crisis, there is sometimes the fear that another shoe will drop, sometime later. To dispel that concern, it is important to be absolutely forthcoming about what might be next. If the reality is more bad news, that should be disclosed. If not, note that as well. People deserve to know the reality of a given situation. The community continually needs to be reminded about the good things and the multiple ways God remains faithful, especially during a crisis.

What Trust Is Not

Sometimes trust can be viewed primarily as transaction or as manipulation. While it is true that trust should be marked by consistency of action, behavior, and performance over time, trust should be based on more than simply a series of transactions and contrived manipulations. Some would propose, "As long as I am given what I want, I will trust you." The opposite of that is, "When you say no to what I want, I will stop trusting."

Healthy relationships are the foundation for trust. As a faculty member once observed, "If we don't know people relationally, how can we trust them?" It is important as leaders to work hard at developing relationships, and to regularly engage in activities that nourish those relationships. We certainly engage in transactions with people as leaders. But the primary motivations behind those transactions should be built on relationships, not the transaction itself.

While eBay, Amazon, or FedEx might be viewed as trustworthy to their hundreds of millions of customers, based primarily on the quality and consistency of their virtual transactions with customers, those rarely are face-to-face encounters. We also know that as soon as those transactions turn sour—as happened with UPS involving the delivery of Christmas packages, or with Carnival Cruise Lines—customers often go elsewhere.

When Mutual Trust Is Not Enough

Building, growing, enhancing, and restoring trust where it is broken remains perhaps the key challenge for effective leaders. It is another soft skill that is indispensable for leadership.[16] As illustrated earlier in my story of closing a campus, mutual trust may not be the antidote that fixes all ills. In other words, the existence of high trust is no guarantee of long-term organizational success. The reality is that there are some decisions that have to be made that aren't precluded by the existence of trust. There are some decisions that

---

PUTTING THE IDEA TO WORK

Leaders need to be diligent in developing and maintaining organizational trust, across multiple constituencies. Regular deposits need to be made into their leadership "I am worthy of your trust" accounts.

- Competent leaders build trust by engaging consistently in repeated acts of integrity, carefully aligning words and actions. Authenticity, candor, and truth-telling are important to building trust, as is their demonstrated competency in the workplace.
- When tough decisions need to be made, the community needs to be assured that the persons affected by the decision were treated fairly.
- Trust can be enhanced through the pursuit and development of healthy mutual relationships. Spending time with, and getting to know, the persons served creates major trust-building capital.

---

have to be made to preserve the mission and the longevity of the organization that may likely damage long-term leadership. Many leaders understand that reality, but they also understand their need as leaders to help ensure the long-term success of the organization.

This may be one of the reasons that executive leadership tenures are often less than ten years across many leadership groups, in both the for-profit and the not-for-profit sector. Those who have long tenures usually serve in organizations where their families have historically dominated the organization, or where the executive either owns the company or is the majority shareholder. Paradoxically, usually most of the employees within organizations other than leadership have far longer employment tenures than the organization's leadership do.

To summarize, effective leaders work at building trust in as many situations as possible. They do so because all of us are created to be people who trust. We *want* to trust. We are created with a bias to trust. We know that when we do, relationships work better and people feel better about themselves and also about the places where they work. That's true whether we're discussing our marriages, our homes, our communities, our politics, or the organizations where we serve.

I saw this often in our students and their eagerness to trust. We had thousands of people in our home every year. The way our home was set up, students were often in the "great room" when we were absent. Yet, after more than twenty thousand visitors, we never had any act of vandalism, intentional destruction, or property damage—the room was always left in perfect condition. Why? We'd like to believe it is because students and others know they were trusted when they were in our home. We often say it this way: "People live up to the expectations you have of them, and if those expectations are not very high, they won't disappoint."

Effective leaders always trust. Why? Because they understand the reality that inspiring trust is job one. As Covey states: "The first thing for any leader is to inspire trust. . . . [T]he truth is that we can establish [trust]. We can grow it. We can extend it. We can restore it. We can become personally and organizationally credible. We can behave in ways that inspire trust."[17]

CHAPTER 8

Ensure Personal and Organizational Accountability

"A body of men holding themselves accountable to nobody ought not be trusted by anybody."

—Thomas Paine[1]

"Man must cease attributing his problems to his environment, and learn again to exercise his will—his personal responsibility in the realm of faith and morals."

—Albert Schweitzer[2]

"Search me, O God, and know my heart; test me and know my anxious thoughts. Point out anything in me that offends you, and lead me along the path of everlasting life."

—Psalm 139:23–24

Three bedrock concepts are necessary for leaders to properly understand the idea of personal and organizational accountability.

The first concept is trustworthiness, or "deserving of trust or confidence." This is the adjectival version of the concept discussed in the previous chapter. In the world of philanthropy, for example, people who donate to an organization must first share the belief that those who lead it are trustworthy. An organization cannot have the reputation for being trustworthy without having trustworthy leaders.

The second concept is that leaders must understand their primary purpose—or more specifically, the ultimate purpose of the organization they lead. What is the purpose for the organization in the first place? Is the purpose to provide for the common good? To make money for the shareholders? To change lives? To educate? To help people make more money? When leaders are unclear about the primary reason their organization exists, they run the risk of what has been called "mission drift."[3] The organization may continue, but in terms of the organization's primary purpose, it now looks dramatically different from what was intended by its founders. Lack of clarity about primary purpose makes organizational clarity more difficult, because the public may be confused about what accountability should look like.

The third concept connected to personal and organizational accountability is the issue of personal motivation. This focus addresses the reason why leaders want to lead in the first place. Is it for fame and fortune? Adulation from those being led? To enjoy power, position, and the financial benefits?

There is a connection between these three concepts that ultimately speaks to personal and organizational accountability. When there is alignment between all three of these concepts, a leader's effectiveness is enhanced. Several biblical stories illustrate this.

Trustworthiness

The first concept, trustworthiness, is illustrated in the biblical story about King Josiah (2 Chron. 24), who served as king for more than three decades. He is described as one who "did what was pleasing in the Lord's sight. . . . He did not turn away from doing what was right." One of his first tasks as a leader was to repair the Lord's temple.

THE CHAPTER IDEA

Soft-skill leaders embrace the need for personal and organizational accountability—not because the law demands it, but because accountability is an important part of integrity. Not only that, but accountability nurtures integrity throughout the organization.

Accountable leaders understand that that the primary purpose of their leadership is to *pursue ends that help achieve the mission of the organization and serve its people*, not the leader's own interests.

They pursue leadership with the *right motivation*, not for purposes of power or selfish gain, but because there is alignment between their leadership role and their commitment to accountability and integrity.

Perhaps the best candidate for leadership is the reluctant leader—someone who is fully qualified to serve but who doesn't need the leadership role to feel good about themselves. These types of leaders understand the important but subtle difference between stating "I *am* the president" and "I *serve* as president."

Leaders sometimes link their personal identity to their leadership position, to the detriment of both the leader and the organization. And sometimes leaders make the wrong decision because it is the popular choice, rather making the difficult choice because it is the one that better serves the mission.

The king had been deeply grieved because of abandonment by his predecessors of a historically well-established practice of temple worship. So he set about the task, in contemporary leadership language, of realignment—that is, correcting and restoring worship practices to what the nation's early leaders had envisioned for the nation he was now leading. Josiah's task was to repair the temple—the physical structure within which the values and symbols of his leadership were to reside and be kept on display.

Every organization has these kinds of symbolic structures, whether located within a website or a building, or on letterhead or a flag. Those symbols and structures give meaning and help define an organization. Repair always costs something, including money, so Josiah engaged in a massive fundraising campaign to enable the repair project to continue.

The story of Josiah's effort includes this interesting observation about those he hired to do the construction work: "But no accounting is to be required from them for the money put into their hands since they work with integrity."[4] No accounting? No performance bond? That is almost unheard of in our bureaucratic, SEC/IRS Form 990 world. Clearly, the workers selected for this project had earned the trust of the king and his leadership team. It is just as clear that they had a reputation for integrity. The people were trustworthy.

So, how does an organization and its people develop this kind of reputation for integrity? Are there skills and practices that help? More on this later.

Primary Purpose

The second concept, primary purpose—the idea that explains what an organization wants to accomplish—is illustrated by a second biblical story, this one about King David. His name was honored not only because of his fame as the primary author of the Psalms, but also for his exploits in leadership. His preparation for leadership took place not in the halls of the leading business schools of his time but in the pasturelands where his vocation, initially, was as a shepherd. Although he had "feet of clay," as illustrated by moral failure in his affair with Bathsheba, he understood from the beginning the primary purpose for his leadership.

King David understood that he had been given his leadership assignment, not for the betterment of his own career, not for building his reputation or brand, not for the financial feathering of his nest, but rather for the care, protection, betterment, and the advancement of the people he was given to lead: "And David realized that the Lord had confirmed him as King . . . and had blessed his kingdom for the sake of his people."[5] He understood that his primary purpose was to help the citizens of his nation to flourish, not in a self-centered way, but rather in a way that helped them understand the importance of their service to and worship of God.

Personal Motivation

The third concept deals with the personal motivation of the leader. Trustworthiness speaks to the "how" of leadership, how leaders lead. Do they lead in such a way that makes them trustworthy? Is the organization known for having trustworthy people? Primary purpose speaks to what the organization does and why it exists. Motivation goes to the reason I aspire to leadership in the first place. Is it because it allows me the opportunity to exercise power and control? Is it because it provides me the opportunity to be a big shot? Sometimes I hear leaders say, "That would be my dream job." Why? The answers all speak to motivation.

As an example, one of the ways to test motivation is to ask this type of question: Why am I considering this position? Would I have been eager to consider pursuit of a comparable position at a much smaller, less well-known place?

When I announced our decision to leave the presidency of the American Bible Society, well-intended "close friends" advised us not to do so because they saw such a move as a "step down" in our career progression. The reasons behind the answer to these types of "step up, step down" questions speak powerfully about personal motivation.

Just as the story of King David illustrates primary purpose, his story also illustrates the issue of personal motivation. Time and again he wrestled with this issue; his words constantly pointed in the direction of desiring a pure heart, a heart in which there was no guile, a pure heart within which to frame his leadership role. One of his more famous observations on this point is his prayer in his 139th Psalm: "Search me, O God, and know my heart; test me and know my anxious thoughts. Point out anything in me that offends you, and lead me along the path of everlasting life."[6]

These three concepts—trustworthiness, primary purpose, and one's personal motivation for leading—are essential aspects of the many soft skills, behaviors, and perspectives that point in the direction of accountability. How do leaders operationalize these realities in their own lives, and in the lives of the people within the organization they lead?

Authentic Motivation and Authentic Primary Purpose Enable Organizational Integrity

I want to begin with personal motive. As noted about the leadership of King David, it is important to approach leadership with the right motive. One of the tough questions those considering organizational leadership should ask is this: Why do I want to pursue a leadership position in the first place? I talk to a lot of students who tell me that their aspirational goal is to one day be a university president. That, of course, is a worthy goal. But why do they aspire to this? What is their motivation? Is it to reap the benefits of a nice compensation package? A more-than-comfortable place in which to live? Because the position comes with elements of visibility, both positive and negative? Because others will be impressed? All of these questions speak to motivation and address why we aspire to leadership.

There are, of course, many benefits to being an organizational leader,[7] but few people consider the downsides. For instance, a demanding travel schedule often frustrates the pursuit of normal friendships and, for us at least, regular Sunday church attendance and participation. Likewise, the practice of regularly attending and participating in small church home group meetings simply doesn't happen. Many organizations reference their special communities, but the reality is that many senior leaders are simply kept on the outside, seldom invited to become a part of what have often been longstanding small groups. This reality is totally understandable, of course. I have discussed this with many leaders throughout several decades, and while there are exceptions, many of them understand and know this reality. Oftentimes lasting friendships, geographically speaking, are away from where the leadership assignment is being carried out.

Further, difficult decisions are part of leadership. Though one's spouse is not involved in those difficult decisions, particular decisions involving personnel are often viewed by others as if the spouse had been complicit in them. As a result, the spouse is often the target for criticism, shunning, or anger. My wife Marylou notes that it's during those times that she thinks she ought to wear a shirt with the words: "It wasn't my decision; talk to my husband." Being the spouse of a leader has its own joys and difficulties.[8]

There is also the perception of living in a fishbowl, where leaders and their families are always on display, and where there can never be an off moment. During my first presidency we had young children, all under the age of ten. How they were dressed, how they behaved in school, their table manners, and how they performed academically were all subjects for regular community discussion. It simply came with the leadership territory.

The stress and the strains of leadership positions sometimes flow into marriage and family relationships. There can be "success" in the leadership role, yet failure in the roles of spouse and parent. Sadly, failed marriages, divorce, and broken homes can be the result. John O'Neill said it this way: "Our society is filled with leaders who have won at work while losing in life."[9] It is important to look ahead—to consider the pluses and minuses of a leadership position, and to commit to putting the necessary guardrails in place to ensure success. The benefits of leadership are often insufficient to compensate for relational family loss, especially tragic loss and devastation.

I've often said that sometimes the best leaders are the reluctant leaders. Reluctant leaders are those who believe they can capably perform at the next level, but knowing the price to be paid by doing so, are reluctant to pay that price. It is often these people who make the best leaders. Why? Because reluctant leaders are people who do not need to be in the next level of leadership in order to know meaning and purpose in their lives, or fulfillment in their calling and vocation. Because they are confident and fulfilled in their current roles, they have no need for nor aspire to rise to the next level of climbing whatever career ladder they are on. Indeed, often they count the cost and conclude that it's simply not worth it. (For "ladder-climber" types, a willingness for someone not to aspire to the next level of leadership is seldom viewed as a positive and almost always as a negative—"no ambition" is the conclusion usually drawn.)

Further, because they are reluctant leaders, if they eventually do serve in a leadership role, they are willing to do the right thing, to make the difficult decision even though it may be unpopular. They do the right thing for the organization even if it's an unpopular decision. They are reluctant to make the wrong decision just to keep their position, because they don't need the higher-level position in order to be fulfilled.

One of our friends in politics put it this way: "To serve in Congress effectively, you have to be prepared to face the reality of losing the next election. Otherwise, you'll soon start focusing on making the decisions that will keep getting you elected instead of making the tough decisions that are in the best interests of the country." This friend served four terms, and then lost his fifth election. He told me, "I was elected with the consent of the people, and I was retired the same way."[10] I've known other leaders particularly near the end of their leadership assignment who questioned whether or not they made decisions to ensure their popularity and legacy, rather than making the decision that was in the best interests of serving the mission—perhaps damaging their legacy. These are always gut checks for leaders, and they speak not only to motivation but also to the issue of how leaders define trustworthiness.

Organizations are blessed to have leaders who have pure motivations for wanting to be in their leadership role. They are blessed further when those same leaders understand that the primary purpose for serving is more about the organizational mission and its people than it is about themselves. That combination of pure motivation and primary purpose contributes significantly to the presence of organizational trustworthiness.

Personal and Organizational Accountability

Say that an organization now has in place a leader with pure motives, who understands an organization's primary purpose, and who seeks to be trustworthy. How does that kind of a leader go about ensuring personal and organizational integrity? I believe the key is the commitment of the leader to insist on authentic personal and organizational accountability.

Leaders need to be willing to place themselves in a position to ensure that others, not just themselves, have a role to play in helping them to be accountable. Leaders must listen to, and seek, the insight and feedback of others within the organization. If they don't, they will often end up creating a false reality of their effectiveness as leaders. That often leads them to make poor choices for themselves and the organization. It is important to be open to others in this way to lead effectively. Listening to and getting feedback from others is also an important element of proper governance in an organization. It is equally important in personal and family roles and relationships.

All leaders must be able to answer this question, "Who can say no to me and make it stick?"—in both their personal and organizational lives. If the answer is "nobody," then my observation of leaders across three decades suggests that they are likely to be headed for trouble—they just don't know it yet.

While accountability in leadership is not a guarantee of success, seldom have I seen success without some kind of accountability system and structure in place. Effective leaders welcome, rather than resist, appropriate accountability. They become better leaders because of it.

Feedback Is an Essential Element of Personal and Organizational Health.

Wise leaders embrace and welcome feedback, even criticism, about whether or not they are effective as leaders. It is strange perhaps that I begin with this observation because it is probably the last thing readers want to hear, especially if the word criticism is used instead of feedback. But interestingly, both the leadership literature and biblical insight point in this same direction—wise leaders embrace and seek feedback. They proactively seek the insight and input of others regarding the effectiveness of their performance.

In reviewing the literature, two writers seem to be particularly perceptive on this topic, Sheila Heen and Douglas Stone.[11] They believe that feedback is essential for effective leadership, but further note that traditional structured organizational feedback systems simply don't work. Why? Only a minority of managers actually complete feedback evaluations, and a majority of those receiving feedback claim it is inaccurate and not helpful. Further, even more managers have difficulty giving feedback or doing coaching.[12] What is going on here? If the giving and receiving of feedback is important, yet the feedback process is broken, then one important piece to help ensure organizational accountability is broken.

According to Heen and Stone, the reality is that people simply don't like to receive feedback, and that includes leaders: "[W]e've found that almost everyone, from new hires to C-suite veterans, struggles with receiving feedback. A critical performance review, a well-intended suggestion or an oblique comment . . . can spark an emotional reaction, inject tension into the relationship, and bring communication to a halt." Further, "improving the skills of the feedback giver won't accomplish much if the receiver isn't able to absorb what is said. It is the receiver who controls whether feedback is let in or kept out, who has to make sense of what he or she is hearing, and who decides whether or not to change."[13] The good news is that both those who give feedback and those who receive it can learn to do this better. But how?

People can handle only so much feedback that's critical at any one time, no matter how helpful or valid. However labeled, feedback is usually viewed as receiving criticism. Again, leadership literature suggests that for criticism to be effective, it needs to be given in a ratio of about six parts praise, one part criticism—a 6:1 ratio. If a person only hears critical feedback about his or her work, without also hearing praise for the good he or she is doing, criticism will be ineffective.[14] Givers of critical feedback have an ongoing responsibility to mix in a healthy dose of praise with their feedback to ensure its effectiveness. This requires work and learning. Of course this reality also has relevance to family relationships, as well as for communication between spouses. Receivers of critical feedback, however, also have learning to do.

Heen and Stone note that the ability to receive constructive criticism in the way it is hopefully intended triggers two competing tensions—a desire to learn, compared with a desire to be accepted "just as I am." I remember discussing this tension with a business

leader one time, and his stated reason for not needing to acknowledge criticism and make needed personal changes was his belief that
it was "just the way he was."

The authors note that there are three triggers that the receiver
needs to manage: the truth trigger, the relationship trigger, and the
identity trigger. The truth trigger focuses on the perceived accuracy
of the content communicated: "When assessments or advice seem off
base, unhelpful, or simply untrue, you feel indignant, wronged, and
exasperated."[15] The relationship trigger is "often colored by what
you believe about the giver . . . or you might reject coaching that you
would accept on the merits if it came from someone else."[16] The identity trigger is all about you, the receiver: "Whether the feedback is
right or wrong, wise or witless, it can be devastating if it causes your
sense of who you are to become undone. In such moments, you'll
struggle with feeling overwhelmed, defensive, or off balance."[17]

I have experienced all three of these triggers. The first time I
was evaluated as a president, the bias of my initial reaction was not
in the direction of gratitude for the feedback and what I perceived
to be criticism but rather to assess its merits—what I deemed to be
accurate or inaccurate. Subjectively, I wanted to dismiss the feedback I believed to be off base, rather than consider it objectively. I
also found myself wanting to know who had made the observation,
believing that if they really knew the situation, or me, they would
have perhaps drawn a more informed assessment.

Ultimately, I have had to move to their third trigger and focus
on me. I had to ask the question in this way: "Even if I disagree with
the accuracy of the feedback; even if I have questions about who said
it; might there still be some truth, some insight in the feedback that
would help make me a better person, a better leader?" That became
the insight gained from my earlier referenced story of standing in
front of the university group, ultimately leading to improvements in
my leadership.

As I have learned, personal and organizational accountability are inextricably connected, and they influence the way critical feedback is sometimes given and often received. That complicates meaningful accountability. How can the tension between accountability and feedback be mediated? In other words, how can accountability on the one hand and critical feedback on the other work hand in hand to be effective? Heen and Stone suggest several things.

First, we have to "know our tendencies."[18] For instance, based on what I know about myself, which of the three triggers just referenced fit what I experience when I receive feedback? And then knowing them, how can I build a check into my own mental feedback processing apparatus, so that I don't color or marginalize its benefit.

Second—and this is no surprise—we need to "disentangle the what from the who."[19] Husbands and wives often do this to each other. There was a point in our marriage when I tended to be dismissive when my wife Marylou raised a concern—not because the feedback was bad, but because it came from someone who was supposed to love me, not criticize me. I was unable to see how her wise counsel actually was a form of love and would help make me a better leader. I needed to ask the question of myself: Would I listen better to these words if they came from someone else? If so, then I had confused the *what* with the *who*.

Third, we need to "find the coaching in criticism."[20] Often the leader's reality is colored because of the difficulty of getting beyond evaluation to coaching: "Some feedback is evaluative; some is coaching. Everybody needs both. Evaluations tell you where you stand, what to expect, and what is expected of you. Coaching allows you to learn and improve and helps you play at a higher level." We need to assume the best, not the worst, in what we hear. As our authors tell us: "Work to hear feedback as potentially valuable advice from a fresh perspective rather than as an indictment of how you've done things in the past."[21]

Fourth, we can think through or "unpack the feedback." The idea is simply to think about it further. Often, in thinking about the events triggering feedback we get overloaded and merely dismiss feedback as a way to cope. We judge people by what we think they intended in sharing their feedback, rather than focus on how we may have perceived their good intentions.

Fifth, we need to be proactive in seeking feedback—in essence, to "request it." This seems to be counterintuitive when people don't always see the benefit in the criticism, let alone seek it. Leaders need to reach out and begin to ask questions such as, "What's one thing you see me doing . . . that holds me or you back?" They might "ask two or three people each quarter for one thing [they] might work on."[22]

As leaders become more adept at both giving and especially receiving constructive feedback, they will also become more open to embracing an accountability agenda. More than just the leader shouting to the people being led, "Do you hear me?" it should be the other way around, with those being led saying to the leader, "Do *you* hear *us*?" The ideal, of course, is mutual accountability, which has as its foundation the healthy give-and-take of constructive feedback. This is very important to the maintenance of both personal and organizational integrity and accountability.

Biblical Insight

Understanding one's purpose for leading, as well as one's motivation for doing so, are important to help ensure accountability and integrity. The Scriptures illustrate that the marks of healthy leadership include a willingness, if not an eagerness, to seek the kind of critical feedback we've been discussing:

> People who accept discipline are on the pathway to life,
> but those who ignore correction will go astray (Prov. 10:17).

To learn, you must love discipline; it is stupid to hate correction (Prov. 12:1).

Fools think their own way is right, but the wise listen to others (Prov. 12:15).

Commit yourself to instruction; listen carefully to words of knowledge (Prov. 23:12).

To one who listens, valid criticism is like a gold earring or other gold jewelry (Prov. 25:12).

Let the godly strike me! It will be a kindness! If they correct me, it is soothing medicine. Don't let me refuse it (Ps. 141:5).

Paradoxically, these teachings suggest that rather than being hesitant to receive critical feedback, leaders ought to run to it, not from it, and seek it eagerly. Indeed, doing so is a mark of those who are wise. There is an important link between accountability and the ability to receive and learn from critical feedback. Effective leaders work hard to establish an organizational climate conducive to healthy give-and-take. Where that exists, both the individuals and the organization have the potential for healthy growth.[23]

The biblical story of King David nicely summarizes these principles. King David was approaching the pinnacle of success in his leadership role—yet violated his commitment to moral integrity and then tried to cover it up with murder and deception (2 Sam. 11–12). Nathan, a member of his senior leadership team, had the courage to confront his leader about his grievous moral failure; and he did so, in essence using words like, "You are the guilty person." The king had caused irreparable harm, and yet rather than rejecting the words of his accuser and condemning him, David acknowledged his guilt and confessed his sin. The words contained in the 51st psalm illustrate the depth of his contrition and plea for God's forgiveness. Nevertheless, David and the nation he led still had to endure the consequences of his wrongdoing.

PUTTING THE IDEA TO WORK

Leaders who champion accountability welcome others to speak into their lives and their performance as leaders. *Every leader must answer the question, "Who can say no to you, and make it stick?"* If the answer is "no one," there is doubtful accountability. Leaders without accountability can be dangerous to the achievement of organizational mission. Championing good governance is an important way to address this concern.

Leaders need to proactively seek feedback about their performance through practices such as "360 reviews." Some leaders like this process; others don't.

An overreliance on formal evaluation processes, however, can immobilize leaders, as they will be tempted to default in their leadership responsibility in order to get better review marks, rather than doing the right thing for the organization.

This story, involving both personal and organizational culpability, illustrates the soft skill of personal and organizational accountability at work—an accountability fueled by a willingness of someone to courageously engage in the process of providing critical feedback to the king. At the same time, the story illustrates the willingness of the leader to acknowledge wrongdoing, to act on what was received. That combination of the mutual giving and receiving of critical feedback is what helps ensure both personal and organizational accountability in leadership.

Feedback itself usually provides further insight about leaders. For instance:

- The *truth trigger* relates to the accuracy or truthfulness of the feedback.
- The *relationship trigger* identifies whether the feedback comes from a reliable source.
- The *identity trigger* affects the ability of the leader to handle feedback, as it may strike in hurtful ways at the leader's identity.

Scripture provides a never-ending stream of passages that identify the need to welcome correction and to respond properly, with gratitude. The evaluation process may be a situation when it is more blessed to receive than to give.

Properly motivated and trustworthy leaders who understand their primary purpose for leading, and who welcome corrective feedback, enhance their ability to embrace personal and organizational accountability.

CHAPTER 9

Embrace the Power of Forgiveness

"If you forgive those who sin against you, your Heavenly Father will forgive you. But if you refuse to forgive others, your Father will not forgive your sins."

—Matthew 6.14-15

"Even if that person wrongs you seven times a day and each time turns again and asks forgiveness, you must forgive."

—Luke 17:4

"He who cannot forgive breaks the bridge over which he himself must pass if he would ever reach heaven; for everyone has need to be forgiven."

—George Herbert[1]

Forgiveness is a word usually associated with a religious context—for instance, God forgiving us for our sins and people forgiving one another. But we do not often see that word referenced in organizational or political discussion. In one of our trips to East Asia, we did hear political discussion about the need for forgiveness between cultures and countries.

In a religious context, forgiveness is referenced as part of the discussion about personal salvation and the need to experience

God's forgiveness, primarily between God and the individual. Once in a while a sermon is preached that calls for forgiveness to be practiced in a horizontal way, that is, from person to person. Usually, though, that horizontal context is limited primarily to situations and circumstances outside of the workplace.

I believe that forgiveness has a role to play in the life of an organization as well, not just in a vertical context with regard to one's relationship to God. Forgiveness applies horizontally, person to person, outside of the workplace—but is also relevant horizontally, position to position, and across every level of the workplace.

It is essential that leaders and the people being led possess forgiving hearts, or at least an inclination in that direction. Colleagues at work who are filled with anger and resentment toward their colleagues not only are less effective workers, but also create risks in the workplace—sadly, sometimes expressed as workplace violence. Having a forgiving heart is fundamentally important for people working together in order to achieve the goal of a healthy, effective, and safe workplace. It is important that leaders champion and model forgiveness at every turn.

Former CEO Walter Wright notes that, unfortunately, "there is little in the management literature about forgiveness. This [forgiveness] may well be the crisis of leadership today. I am becoming increasingly convinced that there can be no leadership without forgiveness. Leadership requires forgiveness and forgiveness nurtures leadership."[2]

Why is practicing the soft skill of forgiveness critical for leadership and organizational effectiveness? Further, what might that look like in organizations?

The Role of Forgiveness in Organizational Life

I was first introduced to this concept of organizational forgiveness when I was in law school. There were regular major student disruptions on the campus in those days. We often arrived at school to observe the next-door administration building surrounded by police in full riot gear. We would walk by vacant lots, where dozens of students were making bandages in anticipation of bloodshed. At the end of a tumultuous semester, given regularized and repeated campus chaos, university leadership made the decision to give all students the simple option to take a "pass" for a given course, rather than the usual letter grade. The intent behind that action was to extend a kind of a university-wide forgiveness to those whose grades were arguably adversely impacted because of the rioting students. Students with failing grades could take a pass instead of the F. Students were extended mercy, in that they did not get what otherwise they might have deserved.

The most visible political example of our generation observing forgiveness was when President Gerald Ford extended a pardon to disgraced former president Richard M. Nixon. In fact, by removing the threat of future governmental consequence, Nixon was actually given more than forgiveness. But more on that later.

From their perspective, leaders understand the realities of the no-holds-barred challenges from disgruntled stakeholders. If taken personally, and if piled one on top of the other, the emotional and related baggage becomes personally unsustainable, immobilizing any attempt at leading. In the Bible, the apostle Paul talked about "daily" carrying the burdens for all the churches. Every leader knows Paul's reality of daily carrying heavy burdens. In 1 Peter 5, the apostle Peter talked about casting his burdens on the Lord—"casting all your cares upon Him, knowing He cares for you." Practicing forgiveness is one of the ways leaders free themselves from the accumulated baggage of the multiple hurts and harms experienced—hurts and harms that might otherwise immobilize them.

I have also learned over the years that sometimes the complaints, the darts hurled, the lawsuits filed, tended to focus on the office held (the office of the president) rather than on the person occupying that office. Talk to people who retire after many years

---

THE CHAPTER IDEA

The idea of forgiveness is prominently referenced in Scripture, often as its key theme. Scripture discusses forgiveness both vertically (between God and humankind) and horizontally (between person and person).

- Leaders need to understand the concept of forgiveness as a cultural value that needs to be embedded in the culture of an organization. Both leaders and those being led are mistake-prone, imperfect people who will regularly disappoint. Without forgiveness, there will be failure.
- Grace and mercy need to mark organizational culture, because people in every part of the organization stand in need of some kind of forgiveness.
- Understanding forgiveness—especially the idea of a forgiveness cycle—is an important part of understanding leadership.

---

of CEO service and one of the reasons given for retirement, and the smiles on their faces, is that they no longer have to carry the stresses and strains of the office. As they leave office, subsequent occupants of the position become the recipients of the nasty letters, or the objects of the lawsuits filed.

Just as those in leadership have a responsibility to extend forgiveness to those who have missed the mark of achieving organizational expectations, it also works the other way around, or at least it should. Sometimes staff need to extend forgiveness to those in leadership who have failed them. Why?

Again, Wright offers a helpful perspective: "The crisis of leadership . . . is a crisis of forgiveness. Leaders are expected to lead without mistakes. There is very little tolerance for error in our organizations, very little acknowledgement of the human limitations of leaders. Organizations want leaders whom they can place before them to bear the burden of decision without error. [Yet] errorless leadership is an oxymoron."[3] As a faculty member once shared with me, "We tend to make our mistakes from within the safety of the classroom, not, as in your case, in full view of everyone in the audience outside of it."

Every leader has dealt with organizational failures or mistakes. All leaders have their wish lists of do-overs. All leaders wish they had evaluated some risks more thoroughly, raised more money, generated more profit, provided better financial margins, and engendered higher morale. Every leader knows the reality of "botched" personnel decisions—poor hires who end up costing the organization much more than just lost salary.

Persons hired who don't work out are not just organizational misses. Rather, their failure should set off alarm bells of a possible systems failure, triggering questions such as: Where were we not as thorough as we should have been in the hiring process? What could we have found out, had we dug deeper and been more persistent? Where should we have resisted more the various pressures to fill vacant positions? Every leader has likely experienced the pain of closing the department, the school, or perhaps a location because of ineffectiveness or the absence of financial viability.

The paradox for leaders is that those being led desire both leadership perfection as well as vulnerability in their leaders. Followers need to know their leaders are real, authentic persons. But every leader knows the reality of having shared too much, of having been too vulnerable. There is a fine line that leaders need to walk, and they have to get that balance right.

In essence, everyone in organizational life stands in need of forgiveness of some type, leaders *and* followers. As Wright observes: "Forgiveness may be the most important gift an organization can give its leaders, and the most important gift a leader can give to its people for whom he or she is responsible."[4]

Some people reading this will argue that forgiveness in the context of an organization should not be a soft skill to be practiced, because it is simply not practical. For example, does the organization simply forgive and forget the act of embezzlement in the finance area? What about the employee who fraudulently created a fabricated false "resume," or the one who withheld material information during an employment interview? What about the student or faculty member who plagiarized the work of another? What about the person who has abused others repeatedly through some assigned position of power or engaged in sexual harassment?

Am I suggesting everyone simply forgives and forgets? The quick answer is no, as we just saw in the previous chapter that even though he experienced grave consequences, King David had also been forgiven. So then, what do we mean by forgiveness? What is its relationship to confrontation? What about restoration and restitution? Each of these four concepts is related to, and is part of, what I call the forgiveness cycle.

The Forgiveness Cycle

There are at least four parts or phases to the forgiveness cycle. I present them here in a kind of linear format, although they are more nonlinear in practice: confrontation, forgiveness, restoration, and restitution. As each part is discussed, stories and/or principles from the Bible will be referenced. That's quite appropriate given the spiritual or transcendent realities that are usually essential for forgiveness to be a reality, both individually and organizationally.

Phase One: Confrontation

An important part in any discussion of forgiveness is the concept of confrontation. Why is it important for effective leadership?

Anyone connected to any organization is a person under another's authority or responsibility for work to be done. A president/CEO is accountable to a governing board as well. It is well known in governance that the first item on the agenda of any university governance board is whether to retain or to conclude the service of the president/CEO. In turn, vice-presidents are accountable to the president/CEO and so on throughout the organization. There is "line accountability" for every person in organizational life. In addition to line accountability, there is also mission accountability. This broadens the scope of responsibility to multiple organizational stakeholders. What happens when an organization falls short in terms of the delivery of its mission? What happens when an individual's work effort simply misses the expected deliverable? What is the gap between the expected versus the actual performance?

This is where confrontation comes in. Make no mistake, confrontation presupposes standards and expectations of some kind. In other words, people need to know—indeed, deserve to know in advance—what the expectations are for their success. Not only that, they need to have a good idea of how the work they do contributes to organizational mission fulfillment. In essence, people need to know in advance what success looks like, in order for their supervisor to conclude that they had a successful year.

The first phase of confrontation has to do with the provision of clearly communicated performance expectations in advance of evaluation. These expectations set the standards for expected performance (if they are not, then that is the place to start). But assuming those are in place, then what?

Part of establishing an organizational culture of forgiveness is to establish the expectation that no one is above being held accountable for performance. In some situations, there appears to be uneven accountability, where the concern for accountability goes in only one direction. Take governing boards, as an example—sometimes a board is more interested in its insistence on staff accountability than it is willing to hold itself accountable for its actions.

When our senior leadership team went through 360-type evaluations, it was important that I, as president, modeled this first. The results of the evaluator went first to the board, but then I also shared evaluations with our leadership team. Then, senior leadership also went through this process, helping to establish an overall commitment to accountability and high performance. Obviously, a "360 evaluation" identifies issues that also need to be corrected and addressed. The results provide a beginning point for meaningful dialogue and discussion. Without clearly communicated expectations or standards of performance of the one being confronted, though, it will be difficult to perform or engage in meaningful confrontation.

The purpose of confrontation is not to catch people doing something wrong. Rather, it is to confirm that people are on the right path—and if they are not, to help them get back on the path. Again, given the reality in the organizational context that people want to succeed and flourish in their work (if done well), they'll appreciate the helpful correctives that will lead to enhanced effectiveness and improved performance. This is called formative confrontation. (Alternatively, appropriate confrontation that helps to enable employees who demonstrate consistently by their work that they really ought to be somewhere else—in some other position or place of employment—is called summative confrontation.)

How do people go about confrontation? One way to get at this is to review the options that we have seen practiced in a variety of contexts.

The "ignore it" option. In this option, one simply ignores bad behavior of any kind. The attitude is something like, "Well, they'll eventually grow out of it or it will stop or they will show improvement so we won't have to address it now." My experience is that rarely happens. The "ignore it" option is often practiced by those who desire conflict avoidance and want to keep the peace at any cost. Bad behavior or poor performance is usually not self-corrected. To ignore it is at the cost of potential negative organizational impact.

The compromise option. With this option, everyone walks away with something, with maybe not the whole loaf but at least with something. The result might be a 70:30 reality or even a 50:50 one. But the problem with this option is that often the real issues are never addressed, paving the way for ultimate subsequent potential disaster.

Prior to the economic collapse of late 2008 and thereafter, the "big three" car companies were often victims of this compromise strategy—usually unions and management were in agreement and each walked away with something but seldom were the big issues addressed. As we now know, both entities thereafter imploded and needed to start afresh.

The "winner take all" option. I've seen this option more often in North American organizations—as compared with, say, Asian organizations—and perhaps the reason relates to historical stories coming out of the "wild, wild West." In this option, there is no shared compromise. Rather, the winner takes everything, from the results of card games to winning gunfights. The concern with this option is that it is usually accompanied with, and driven by, the power-holders. In the organizational context—be it senior leadership, coaches, supervisors, or faculty holding the power card of a good grade—there is always the possibility of using a position of power to achieve a given objective. That is often what leads to abuse and other hurtful behaviors. Ironically, even in the military we're beginning to see approaches to leadership other than simple reliance on one's power card. I'm reminded of the Lord Acton quote: "Power corrupts, and absolute power tends to corrupt absolutely."

Each of the above options may be helpful in a particular situation, as a way to approach confrontation. If in doubt as to where to begin the forgiveness cycle, start with the first step: meaningful confrontation. To make clear for all parties, from the beginning, what is expected in terms of both relationships and performance is the place to begin. To identify clearly for employees those behaviors or the issues of concern that are at variance from a previously communicated expected behavior or performance, and to do so in a timely way, is ultimately a good thing even if it is a hard thing.

Surprisingly, one of the complaints people have about their jobs and their employer is that they rarely are given any feedback about their performance, good or bad. And sometimes hearing anything, even a reprimand, is better than hearing nothing. The writer of the Proverbs laments that reality this way: "A spoken reprimand is better than approval never expressed." (Prov. 27:5, MSG). People truly do want to know if they're hitting the standard expected by their employer. I've met very few people who intended to begin their day with words like these: "Today, our plan is to go to work and perform badly." The reverse is almost always the case.

If asked, persons would probably respond that they don't relish confrontation by a supervisor. That's because many times the word "confrontation" has a pejorative sound to it—and further, because people have seen it modeled in pretty ugly ways. What if confrontation took place within a context of trust, with the intent of helping, of bringing clarity to one's performance? What if it were done in real time, rather than reserved for the annual performance review?

Confrontation is not easy nor painless, particularly when it may lead either to job change or person change. But how confrontation is done often sets the context within which the hard work of seeking forgiveness takes place.[5]

Phase Two: Redemptive Forgiveness
There are multiple key words which need to be part of any vocabulary in the discussion of the soft skills of leadership—words such as

"faith," "love," and "hope"; as well as words like "learner" and "team player." The word "forgiveness" is another. However, I've found it to be among the most difficult to operationalize in leadership assignments. Three examples come to mind that illustrate why.

In *Les Miserables* by Victor Hugo, the leading antagonist is an officer by the name of Javier. He is always interested in the rule of law and justice. He pursues Jean Valjean, who himself has been shown forgiveness. Eventually, Javier captures his fugitive, but at every turn is showered with redemptive forgiveness. Unable to fit the concept of forgiveness within his idea of justice, Javier commits suicide to reconcile what to him becomes irreconcilable. He just could not handle forgiveness, and failed to understand that grace trumps justice.

In the summer of 2012 I was helping lead a leadership development seminar in East Africa for senior government ministers. When I got to this subject of forgiveness, I used the example of Nelson Mandela and his forgiving ways. There was real struggle in our seminar about whether Mandela's way (the Truth and Justice Commission) was the right choice because it did not involve justice. "People should have had to pay for their crimes and not just be forgiven," was the consensus in the classroom. This was the hurdle over which Javier in the previous illustration could never surmount.

Laura Hillenbrand's book *Unbroken* illustrates a third example. She tells the life story of Louis Zamperini, the Olympic distance runner who was denied the chance to set a world Olympic record by the bombing of Pearl Harbor. He later served during WWII and was captured by the Japanese. Hillenbrand recounts Zamperini's horrific multiple-year torture in Japanese prison camps, especially by a tormentor by the name of "the Bird." Near the end of his life, Zamperini, who had been freed from his own hate through God's transcendent forgiveness (experienced through a Billy Graham Crusade in Los Angeles), tried to arrange a meeting in Japan with his primary tormenter to extend him forgiveness. In spite of his

> ## PUTTING THE IDEA TO WORK
>
> *The first part of the forgiveness cycle* is for all to understand the need for mutual confrontation or courageous conversations as a necessary part of organizational culture.
>
> - The attitude that should result from confrontation should be, from the one confronting, carefulness; from the one confronted, gratitude.
> - Forgiving someone is always an act of obedience, and has little to do with feelings or whether the "I'm sorry" is perceived to be genuine and heartfelt.
> - Forgiving someone doesn't automatically lead to reconciliation or restoration, but hopefully that will eventually result, in God's time.
> - The process that may either precede or follow the act of forgiving may be that of restitution. Restitution may be an important element of eventually achieving restoration and reconciliation.

effort to arrange such a meeting, he could never reach him. Eventually Zamperini was able to return to his horrific place of torture in Japan, Sugamo Prison, and to extend forgiveness: "In bewilderment, the men who had abused him watched him come to them, his hands outstretched, a radiant smile on his face."[6] In essence, he was able to let go of that horrible past so that it would no longer hold him as prisoner.[7]

In each of these illustrations—and there are countless others—the reality is that extending forgiveness is hard. It is hard in families, communities, among nations, or within organizations. Forgiveness is counterintuitive. People and organizations that both extend and receive it are forever changed. It is often transformative. So why is it so hard to do?

In the culture of organizations, extending forgiveness is often seen as a sign of weakness, of organizational softness. There are few if any courses in business schools that deal with the subject of forgiveness, and fewer still within our esteemed schools of diplomacy. Given the tension in the US discussion and debate over immigration and amnesty provisions, how long would a global leader last if his or her primary focus on diplomacy was based on the concept of forgiveness? So too with organizations and their leaders. Yet the practice of redemptive forgiveness changes both people and organizations in counterintuitive ways. What, in essence, is forgiveness, and what is it about forgiveness that changes the moment?

In the dictionary sense, forgiveness includes the idea of the "giving up of resentment" or the idea of "granting pardon for or remission of an offense." The concept of mercy—not getting something like a bad consequence that I deserve—is also part of forgiveness. For instance, when President Nixon was extended forgiveness by President Ford, he was also extended mercy, avoiding receipt of far greater consequences that he likely deserved. Presidential pardons extended at the end of a president's term in office provide repeated examples of extending forgiveness. At the same time, grace is receiving something positive that I know I don't deserve. Oftentimes, we are recipients of grace in multiple and undeserving ways. Forgiveness involves both of these concepts—mercy and grace.

Forgiveness often deals with the idea of guilt (I did something bad) and shame (I simply *am* bad). So when somebody approaches me knowing that I had behaved badly, and then counterintuitively extends me grace and says, "You are forgiven" . . . well, it's no wonder Javier couldn't handle it. Even if extended forgiveness, I'm often left with the struggle of forgiving myself. Indeed, all of us—Javier-like—may struggle with this concept of forgiveness.

The greatest teacher the world has ever known is Jesus of Nazareth. His teaching on this subject of forgiveness is powerful. One of my favorite teachings of Jesus on this topic is found in Luke 17. He starts His teaching to His disciples with this simple instruction about confrontation and forgiveness this way: "If you see your friend doing wrong, correct him. If he responds, forgive him. Even if it's personal against you, and repeated seven times throughout the day, and seven times he says, 'I'm sorry, I won't do it again,' forgive him."

Their response to Jesus was interesting: "Give us more faith." Their response was that to show forgiveness in this example was so hard that the only way they could do it was to be granted more faith—hence, their request for "more faith." They believe they needed more faith to extend that kind of forgiveness, especially where the offense was often repeated, intentional, and personal. Our responses would likely be not much different from theirs.

Jesus taught that to extend forgiveness is not an option to consider, but rather a duty to perform. Jesus then followed up this teaching on forgiveness with an illustration, to point out that extending forgiveness repeatedly was not a choice, nor a matter of needing more faith but rather a duty and responsibility. Jesus taught that the employee whose job it was to help care for the farm and help prepare the evening dinner would likely not complain about preparing the family's evening meal after a hard day's work, as he was simply doing his duty as an employee. Jesus then applied the story to the teaching on forgiveness: "When you've done everything expected of you, be matter of fact and say, 'The work is done. What we were told to do, we did.'" No extra credit. Just matter-of-fact obedience of doing one's duty.

To be sure, the story that Jesus told here, along with many others, is connected to the importance of forgiveness. But this story also teaches us something else—that extending forgiveness trumps justice, a concept hard to understand in primarily justice-only motivated cultures. In other words, in this story, Jesus didn't focus on whether the hired man was being fairly treated—or whether it was fair for the master to insist that he, the master, be served food first, ahead of the man who had worked hard in the field all day. No, Jesus focused instead on the servant's responsibility to do his duty. So must we when it involves our responsibility to extend forgiveness to others. What does forgiveness involve? There are at least these three considerations.

First, don't keep bringing up the offense. When forgiveness is extended, one of the things we commit to is not raising the matter again. or at least to trying not to do so. Unfortunately, as one sage has put it: Often when we bury the offense, we put a grave marker by the spot. We keep reminding the offender over and over of the offense. That not only isn't effective in the restorative process but is often very hurtful. Scripture reminds us that when God forgives us, he obliterates the record of the offense.

Second, don't communicate it to others. If the offense has been done in a nonpublic way, we need to seek forgiveness from the affected parties. But if we have been the offended parties, there usually is no need to tell others. In doing so, both the offender and the offended help delay the ultimate hoped-for goal of restoration.

Third, don't dwell on it—let it go and move on. This applies both to the offender and the offended. After forgiveness has been extended, we don't continually dwell on the matter—we move on. This involves letting go of the past. The person who says, "I'll forgive you, but I'll never forget it" has probably not really extended or granted forgiveness. We may have to work hard at getting release from forgetting. Sometimes this will require the help of a counselor or trusted friend.

I was not a regular watcher of Oprah Winfrey when she was on TV, but on one of her shows the topic was forgiveness and about what it means. One of her guests discussed the concept that forgiveness involves the idea of letting go of the past, knowing that it can never be changed. That reality is also a part of what it means to be forgiven.[8] But while the past can't be changed, it can be redeemed.

This was illustrated at Taylor University by the parents of university students who were killed in a tragic semi-trailer truck accident in 2006, who publicly forgave the one responsible for the death of their children. Five lives were lost and one student, badly injured, survived the accident. Five weeks after the accident, however, authorities realized that one person they thought had died was actually the survivor, and that the person who they thought had survived had actually been buried by the wrong family five weeks previously.

The subsequent stories about parental forgiveness by all five affected families of the driver of the semi-truck which had crossed the interstate median—and later, the story of reconciliation and forgiveness between the two families of those involved with the mistaken identity—became a national and international topic of conversation. The story was featured on TV broadcast shows and in print media, and highlighted by NBC broadcast TV anchor Matt Lauer, who discussed it multiple times on both the *Today Show* and on perhaps his highest-ever-rated *Dateline* presentation of the story. This story in part was later memorialized in the *New York Times* bestseller *Mistaken Identity*.[9] All of the families involved in this story learned, and continue to learn, not about forgetting the past but about letting go of the past. In his parable of the unmerciful servant, Jesus addressed these issues in part by stating that forgiveness eventually also has to affect the heart: "That's what my heavenly Father will do to you if you refuse to forgive your brothers and sisters from your heart."[10] This is what all of these marvelous families have done. This is an essential part of forgiveness.

It is necessary to make an important distinction at this juncture. Extending forgiveness does not mean necessarily that there will be no further consequences. Forgiveness and consequences are not mutually exclusive. Just as when a nail is pulled from the wood, the hole that remains does not go away. There is a scar that remains. So too with forgiveness. Just because forgiveness has been extended does not mean that's the end of the story. When a parent forgives a child for inappropriate behavior, that doesn't mean that discipline doesn't follow.

The biblical story of David and Bathsheba, again, illustrates this point. Though he was forgiven by God, there were negative consequences that plagued King David and his family for the rest of his life.[11] Yet even so, God uses all circumstances and situations for His purposes. He makes crooked roads straight and levels mountains and valleys. We all need forgiveness and to move on with life, knowing God has forgiven us. What, then, about the last two phases of the forgiveness cycle—restoration and restitution?

Phase Three: Restoration

If effective confrontation has taken place, and if forgiveness has been extended—better yet, mutually extended—then there is the third step in the forgiveness cycle: pursuing restoration.

Often in the process of confrontation and forgiveness, a rift in relationships may have occurred. In an organization or in a family, steps still have to be taken, to rebuild trust, to see a reputation reestablished. Often a third party may have to get involved to help. Those steps toward restoration take time—years, perhaps.

Once again, King David serves as an example. He and his son Absalom had a severe falling-out, for a grievous family failure (killing his brother)—so much so that Absalom was kicked out of the palace. David didn't see his son for more than two years. Finally, Absalom pursued his father and asked him to bring him back from exile. David reluctantly agreed, but then refused to see his son.[12] Unfortunately, there never was restoration between father and son, which eventually led to civil war. Absalom, the son, was killed in battle, never having been reconciled to his father. Among other things, this illustrates that restoration is not easy and sometimes doesn't work. But shouldn't at least the effort be made?

So too, efforts for restoration should always be pursued between coworkers or friends. In the organizational context, this is also difficult, and many organizations do not extend mercy and grace after forgiving an offense. "You violated our policies, so your employment is terminated." But what would happen, organizationally, if somehow people were given another chance? In higher education, probationary faculty usually have up to six years to demonstrate their full academic competency. If they do not succeed, they are provided one additional transitional year. But often that is not the case with nonfaculty.

In the church structure context, I have often observed very intentional processes established with church leaders who have gone through the confrontation-forgiveness phases. These steps usually involve some time away from workplace assignments, work with a counselor, and perhaps other steps. The goal, though, is to achieve restoration so as to enable the person to get back on track, and to continue with ministry of some kind, either at the former place of employment or someplace else. Perhaps this model needs to be explored more fully in other types of workplaces.

Phase Four: Restitution

Thus far my focus has been on discussing three phases in the forgiveness cycle—confrontation, forgiveness, and restoration. Often that is enough. But sometimes it is not. Why? In some offense-generating situations, property—sometimes tangible and sometimes intangible—is an issue. The focus of restitution is to repair the property damage, to make the damaged person whole. This, too, is part of the forgiveness cycle. Unfortunately, this property or financial part is often not readily acknowledged within organizations, so lawyers and litigation often result.

The biblical story and book of Philemon summarizes and illustrates these multiple phases of the forgiveness cycle. Philemon, a friend of the apostle Paul, suffered two potentially early-century losses when his slave Onesimus fled from his master. Presumably, Philemon was injured through the loss to his workforce, and perhaps also by the loss of property. In that century, being a runaway slave was a capital offense. In the meantime, Onesimus encountered Paul and his Christian teachings and became a follower of Jesus. But Paul was friends now with both Philemon and Onesimus, and Paul realized he had a responsibility to help address this broken relationship. How should he address this issue with his friend Philemon on behalf of Onesimus?

This story is a brilliant case study about how Paul addressed this situation, touching each step of the forgiveness cycle. He confronted his friend Philemon and subsequently counseled forgiveness and restoration, noting that Philemon owed Paul his very life. But then Paul also addressed the restitution piece—"if he owes you anything, charge it to my account." It is sometimes this financial piece that generates considerable relational and organizational tension. But this is the piece that attempts to address the matter of restitution. This, too, is an important and necessary part of the forgiveness cycle.

The effective practice of the forgiveness cycle, both relationally and organizationally, requires soft skills. Effective leaders recognize the important parts that confrontation, forgiveness, restoration, and restitution play in embedding an organizational culture of forgiveness in the places they lead. Why? At some time during their lives every leader has been extended forgiveness or grace in his or her own life. Accordingly, they recognize its transformative power to change and empower lives. They understand that the ones who have been extended forgiveness also need to be its champion, extending it to others. Those who do will be leaders who end up leading special places—places with an organizational culture that is authentic, vulnerable, healthy, and filled with grace.

CHAPTER 10

Follow and Lead, Lead and Follow

"Bookshelves across the nation are filled with 'How-to' books on effective leadership. Few focus on effective followership: To be a great leader, one must first learn to be a dedicated follower. This is as true in military service as it is in corporate America."

—US Military Chaplains Bible[1]

"He who cannot be a good follower cannot be a good leader."

—Aristotle[2]

"If you want to be a great leader, you must first become a great follower."

—Michael Hyatt[3]

◆ Quick: When is the last time you remember attending a Followership Conference? "Never" is probably the likely answer. In more than thirty years of being involved in and doing CEO leadership, I don't ever recall hearing about one. Almost every conference has been focused on leadership—that is, learning how to be a more effective leader. The US culture is obsessed with leadership. In universities the standard adult education degree-completion major is "organizational leadership," and one can get all kinds of graduate degrees in leadership. Every year the billion-dollar "leadership" industry engages millions of people in all kinds of activities, as leadership competence is sought. The assumption, of course, is that if we have the right leaders in place on the right bus and in the right seat[4] and they have the right stuff and lead in the right ways, companies, stockholders, communities, families, citizens, and nations will be better off.

As one writer has observed, "We are a society in love with leadership and uncomfortable with followership, though the subjects are inseparable. We don't honor followership."[5] Paradoxically, all leaders know the reality that they "are almost never as much in charge as they are pictured to be, followers almost never are as submissive as one might imagine."[6]

The leadership issue is a simple one: Can there be leaders if there are no followers? "There is no leader without at least one follower. . . . Yet the modern leadership industry is built on the proposition that leaders matter a great deal and followers hardly at all."[7] Leaders and followers, it turns out, are two different sides of the same entity—like left and right, inside and outside, hot and cold, top and bottom. It takes the opposite word to define the other. Without this understanding of leadership, the organization ride will indeed be a bumpy one, with little ultimate ownership of overall organizational goals and objectives. In essence, there can be no effective leadership without effective followership.

The terms "leader" and "follower" are not merely titles in a job description or personality types. Rather, they are "distinct roles that executives and managers are called upon to play. One is the role of leader in their own right. The other is the role of courageous follower."[8]

This, then, is a leadership paradox. If there is no leadership without followership—and if the primary focus of leadership development is not on developing followers but leaders—then what happens to the assumption that effective leaders will solve problems that need to be solved, fix the things that are broken, and identify the opportunities waiting to be discovered? Where does a focus on followers fit into the leadership discussion?

Thankfully, effective leaders have always understood the importance of just how essential followers are in leading an enterprise. They understand that, if organizations are to be fully effective, they have to be led in such a way that empowers followers to do what they must do. So then, what must followers do?

Followers as Leaders

First, followership is not a passive act, nor is leadership only an active one. I have seen the critically important roles played by followers in helping to keep organizations vibrant and flourishing and out of trouble. "There's a cultural misconception that following is a passive act. It's not. It's a partnership that recognizes different responsibilities while working toward a common goal. . . . Traditional leadership theory puts the responsibility for the leader-follower relationship with the leader. In my observation, it often works the other way around."[9] In reality, "[I]t is the quality of the relationship of leaders and followers, all the way up and down the organization chart, that makes or breaks organizations."[10]

Second, effective followers empower leaders by giving their work legitimacy and ownership. Simply put: Without the blessing and support of followers, leaders would be ineffective: "Followers have about as much influence on their leaders as their leaders have on them. Leaders cannot maintain authority . . . unless followers are prepared to believe in that authority. In a sense, leadership is conferred by followers."[11] The contrasting stories in the Bible about Rehoboam and Jeroboam illustrate this.[12]

Rehoboam, as the son of Solomon, was the presumptive next leader of Israel. Jeroboam and his leadership group were, in essence, asked by Rehoboam and his leadership to fall in line and be good followers of the new king. Rehoboam was asked about his leader-ship philosophy—and once that was (poorly) communicated, he was deserted by Jeroboam: "So the king did not listen to his followers [to the people]. . . . When all Israel saw that the king refused to listen to them [his followers], they answered the king: 'What share do we have in David, what part in Jesse's son?'" So they departed and went another way.

Whereas followers in organizations usually don't have the option to leave their employment as Jeroboam did, many sometimes simply check out from giving the organization their best effort. They remain, but their focus becomes "polishing their invisibility" within the organization rather than full pursuit and enhancement of its mission.

"Polishing their invisibility" is a phrase I learned while living in New York City. Employees used it to describe their utter detachment from the mission of their employer, coupled with only a marginal commitment to doing their work—to do just enough to get by. People who were working at polishing their invisibility seldom volunteered to do anything more than their jobs; they avoided eye contact with their colleagues; they were the last to arrive and the first to leave; and they were often the first to criticize and complain. Unfortunately, their numbers may be many within organizational life.

Third, followers serving in a senior leadership capacity have special obligations to their direct reports to help hold them and the organization to high standards of performance. Sometimes "the orientation of those around the leader often becomes personal sur-vival instead of group optimization. Optimum group performance requires both leaders and followers [to] place the organization's welfare at least on par with protecting their personal interests." Followers who serve as senior leaders cannot let "their needs for physical security and social acceptance outweigh pride in organiza-tional achievement. Instead of risking the conversations needed to address leadership's own contributions to mediocre performance, they 'play the game' and conform, regardless of the cost to the organization."[13] In essence, when followers fail to do their job, they are also contributing to organizational failure: "Good constituents produce good leaders. They not only select good ones (think interview committees), they make them better by holding them to standards of performance."[14] Some have referred to these conversations as courageous conversations.

In organizations, however, courageous conversations are usually thought of as being led by the leader. What I have in mind here is the other way around and much more difficult, where followers, either individually or in groups, confront the leader, raising points of concern. Sometimes, because of the fear of losing one's job ("if I do that"), these types of courageous conversations seldom happen. Some leaders discourage it. I once knew a CEO who fired people on the spot if this happened or if they ever mentioned they were thinking about taking a job elsewhere—even for good reasons.

Fourth, followers understand the fundamental difference between holding a position of authority and having subordinates, as compared to being a leader and having followers. As Gardner notes, "The assumption by line executives that . . . they can lead without being leaders is one reason bureaucracies stagnate. They are given subordinates, but they cannot be given a following. Surprisingly, many of them don't know they are not leading. They mistake the exercise of authority for leadership, and as long as they persist in that mistake, they will never learn the art of turning subordinates into followers."[15]

The operative difference between a subordinate and a follower comes down to the words "have to," as compared to the words "want to." Subordinates have to go to work. Followers want to go to work. The task of leaders is to help subordinates make the shift to followership—what Gardner refers to as a leadership art. This leadership art is a soft skill, and its pursuit is no easy quest. It is a necessary one.

Many subordinates are simply waiting to be led in the direction of becoming followers. Effective leaders understand this and behave accordingly. Empowering followers does not mean that leaders are abandoning their assigned leadership responsibilities. Rather, this understanding is a more complete understanding of what followers in any organization essentially desire:

> Followers do like being treated with consideration, do like to have their say, do like a chance to exercise their own initiative—and participation does increase acceptance of decisions. But there are times when followers welcome rather than reject authority, want prompt and clear decisions from the leader, want to close ranks around the leader.[16]

This is especially true at times of organizational crisis, when there is considerable confusion and chaos. The chaos could be the result of financial difficulty, or the convergence of negative external factors such as a court decision or legislative agenda. At Taylor University, it was the result of a tragic van accident that saw the loss of five members of our community. These are the kinds of times when leaders, absorbing the chaos of the hurts and frustrations of those being led, step forward to identify the way ahead and to provide hope.

Leaders as Followers

Ira Chaleff, writing in *Ideas for Leaders*, observes that "we are a society in love with leadership and uncomfortable with followership, though the subjects are inseparable. We don't honor followership. We talk pejoratively of followers being weak individuals. And we certainly don't train staff how to be strong followers."[17] Perhaps we learned this dislike of being followers as children.

Growing up as kids, we played the game "follow the leader." No one ever had to define the term "leader" for us. That wasn't necessary.

THE CHAPTER IDEA

Many people talk about *leadership* but very few discuss the importance of *followership*. The reality is that there can be no leaders if there are not followers. The terms require each other for definition.

Many mistakenly believe that a position of authority makes one a leader. Not so. If you hold a position of authority, you have subordinates, but not necessarily followers. The leadership task is to see a shift from subordinate to follower—from "I *have* to do this" to "I *want* to do this."

A leader is seldom *always* a leader. Rather, a leader also follows, and followers also lead. Effective leaders follow and lead, and lead and follow.

- Effective leaders cultivate the idea that followership is not a passive act, nor is leadership always an active one.
- Effective followers are the ones who give legitimacy to their leaders, and ownership to their work.

We intuitively knew that being the leader was the important role, and being the leader is what we as kids aspired to. The leader was the popular one; the leader was the one those of us in the kid culture looked up to. None of us ever aspired to be the follower; all of us wanted to be the leader. Decades later, not much has changed. Society seems preoccupied with, if not addicted to, this leadership focus—for all kinds of reasons. Yet leaders also need to understand and develop the capacity to follow. What do I mean by this? Organizationally, what might that look like?

There are several ways to approach this topic, in addition to the earlier discussion about the importance of having an organization's followers being prepared to confront and challenge organizational leaders when they miss the mark and fail to get it right. Again, this is the approach represented by a Tom Peters piece, wherein he notes, "Without followers, leaders cannot be challenged."[18] Peters is right in assuming there are times when the leader must be challenged. Part of developing leader-follower capacity, though, is for the leader to invite challenge, and even welcome it.

This highlights my first point: Leader-followers must actively position themselves not only to hear the challenges of followers but also to ensure their regular receipt. To be sure, this is a counterintuitive idea to many leaders, as most of the time leaders only want to hear the good things going on. When the results of a 360 review—one of the ways to get the feedback of followers—are presented, there is usually a bit of defensiveness. Some leaders may actually reject the use of 360 reviews as a way to receive useful feedback.

When I was in graduate school, I remember one particular textbook quote that spoke to this issue: "Few indeed are the organizational disasters that occurred unforeseen by someone [within the organization]."[19] There are those within every organization who see where problems potentially reside and where opportunities are likely to be found. Effective leader-followers understand this reality and regularly structure opportunities to receive this kind of input. Those who don't potentially end up in a fantasyland of their own creation.

The writer of Proverbs calls the listening leader wise: "If you listen to constructive criticism, you will be at home among the wise."[20] Sometimes this means nothing more than creating a culture where people know that their thoughts are not only invited but welcomed. In some organizations, employees are scared to death even to make comments of any kind, let alone ask questions, believing that if they do, their job may be at risk. Nourishing this kind of culture also incentivizes people to identify missed opportunities.

Every organization has a mission statement that it feels pretty good about, yet oftentimes there is opportunity for improvement. We at Taylor University were going through this kind of mission statement review and felt really positive about that part of the statement that talked about "ministering Christ's redemptive love to a world in need." I will always remember the day when a faculty colleague contacted me and suggested that our statement might be made stronger if it were to read: "ministering Christ's redemptive love *and truth* to a world in need." The suggested change is now a very important part of our mission statement.

Second, effective leader-followers intentionally structure appropriate accountability systems around them so that somebody can say "no" to them as they lead. This goes beyond merely structuring opportunities for input. This step calls for structuring an accountability system in which somebody can say "no" to the leader. Developing this kind of system is part of developing the capacity of being a follower.

I remember flying home to New York from a Los Angeles board meeting that had a planned stopover in Chicago. My seatmate on the flight, it turned out, was a management consultant from Princeton, New Jersey. We swapped stories of what we had seen and experienced in various organizations, and we finally got to this question: "What is the one essential question you have found that every effective leader needs to answer?"

His answer was quick and insightful: "Who can say no to you—and make it stick?" His point was that if there is no one who can do this, whether within an organization or outside it, then that leader has no accountability. That's where fault lines eventually develop, which often lead to the destruction or impairment of both the leader and the organization. As already noted, this also is a critical responsibility of followers. To paraphrase Tom Peters, without followers in place who can question and say no to a leader for the right reasons and in the right way, both the organization and its leadership will be headed for difficulty. Wise leaders understand this and seek to build accountability into the organizations they lead.

Third, leader-followers seek input from followers to help compensate for their known blind spots. This idea simply acknowledges the human predicament, that leaders do have blind spots.[21] They simply are not capable of knowing and seeing and anticipating all of the problems and opportunities that will be faced, both internally and externally. That includes leaders' inability to see their own blind spots and those of the organization. Thankfully, people within the organization know these realities and can share them with leaders if asked. So, again, organizations and the leaders within them need to create cultures wherein followers will be able to come forward with their observations and issues of concern. If, however, the leader fails to understand these different leading and following roles, this kind of organizational culture will likely never emerge.

Fourth, leader-followers develop a capacity for understanding the importance of both leading and following as part of their definition of leadership as they do both. A leader both leads and follows, and a follower both follows and leads. In other words, effective leaders are not always leading, and effective followers are not always following. This is true in organizations, within families, and in all other relationships.

Whenever I'm part of a leadership development seminar, whether within the US or in some other part of the world, I usually discuss this topic of leading and following. To gauge an audience's understanding of these two terms, I sometimes place two stacks of different colored baseball caps on tables on opposite sides of the room. One stack has red caps, the other stack has green ones. I tell the audience that the red caps represent the leadership role and the green ones represent the followership role. Then I ask them to participate, asking them to come to the front and pick up the color of the cap that best describes their understanding of their role within the organization in which they serve.

Interestingly, the leadership or red caps disappear pretty quickly while the stack of green followership caps often remains piled high. Rarely does the same person pick up one of each. Yet, that is precisely what I hope for. Indeed, that is the point of the exercise. Effective leaders should be picking up one of each color, as they are constantly putting on and taking off the leadership cap and exchanging it for the followership cap and vice versa. They understand that leading is also about following, and that following is about leading. As stated in the words of Ecclesiastes, there is a time for everything under the sun. There's a time to lead and there's a time to follow. Effective leaders have learned the soft skill, the art of when and how to do each.

Let me illustrate further: I spent more than twenty-five years working with university faculty, all experts in their academic disciplines and all very knowledgeable about curricular matters. When I went to a faculty meeting in which academic curricular matters were being discussed, I quickly grabbed my follower hat. While I understood curricular issues, I clearly was not the expert; I followed their lead and tried to learn more from them about curricular issues, raising questions as might be appropriate. But the faculty members were clearly driving the discussion, not me. My role was to be a follower and to learn from them. If I followed and learned from the faculty, that learning would clearly inform how I would lead. I needed to follow well in order to be an effective leader.

I also worked with a board and served as its sole employee. I was subject to terms of employment completely at its discretion. There usually were communicated expectations of what the board desired from me as their leader, and sometimes those expectations were not always clearly expressed. But rarely was there joy around the board table if I, as president, forgot that my first responsibility was to follow the directions indicated by the board. If there was ambiguity with an assignment, I had the responsibility to seek clarity. My task in navigating my board leadership assignment was to make sure that what I thought I heard the board say was, indeed, what actually was said. A lack of clarity in understanding, coupled with presumption, often can turn deadly for leaders caught in this predicament. Unfortunately, many organizational highways are littered with the leadership wreckage of those who forgot how to follow their board's lead.[22]

Alternately, while my fundamental role as president/CEO was to deliver satisfactorily on assigned objectives, there also was the sense I needed to contribute in helping to lead the board. In the US, governing boards of universities in the independent sector are all part-time volunteers who usually have full-time employment or service elsewhere. As a result, I was the only full-time member of the board, also as an employee, who spent one hundred percent of his time on university issues. Accordingly, the board expected me, as the follower-CEO, to help lead it through the multiple issues the members were considering. In other words: My role was to help prepare and shape the issues in such a way that they, as a part-time governance group, could deliberate responsibly, draw reasonable conclusions, and effectively govern the university. Thus, while I served the board, in some ways I also helped to lead the board.

One time when I was leading a year-long strategic planning exercise, I asked board leadership at the beginning of the assignment what kinds of outcomes they were looking for. Their response? "We don't know, but we'll know it when we see it." So, during the next year, through multiple meetings with various constituent groups, I became a quiet follower, listening, asking questions, and picking up the cues frequently strewn among all of the normal conversations that occur among board members. If I had insisted on being just the leader of that exercise, most likely I'd still be trying to figure out what the board was ultimately seeking. I learned not by leading, but by listening to their words and to their hearts as a follower. As a result, at the end of that year a successful planning effort ultimately emerged, was adopted, and was put in place.

Leaders as Receivers of Feedback

Whereas the focus in this section could easily be on followers as receivers of supervisor feedback, it is necessary also to focus on how leaders receive feedback. How a leader responds to feedback, especially negative or non-affirming feedback, will likely be a predictor of long-term effectiveness. If leaders are not in a position to hear or receive the messages, there will be a problem. Thus, leaders need to face this question directly: "What is your reaction to receiving negative feedback or criticism?" Or further, "How do you react when someone pushes back on what you think are excellent ideas?"

In general, receiving feedback of this type is not always viewed as something to be valued by leaders and, as a result, is seldom sought. In a recent informal survey of college and university presidents, there was strong negative criticism of using 360 reviews to evaluate presidential performance. The frustration is often expressed something like this: "Eighteen pages of charts and graphs and no ability to have follow-up conversations to clarify the feedback."[23] Some leaders adopt the feedback equivalent of "don't ask, don't tell," which means, they don't ask for feedback and seldom proactively put themselves in positions for others to tell them their concerns.

Again, our human bent goes against truly receiving, let alone seeking, criticism. Why? Because we have the emotional need to feel good about who we are. At the same time, we know of our need to "learn and grow"—a value we continually communicate to the organizations we lead. Fortunately, the skills necessary to be better receivers are "distinct and learnable."

The Leadership Challenge and Opportunity

To summarize: There are few books on this subject of the leader-follower relationship, and few courses on this topic fill the curricula of the business schools. As such, the learning that takes place on these subjects is often self-learning, not the result of case studies or book learning. My encouragement is for leader-followers to put in place processes and structures that will improve their ability to be followers, in whatever ways they can. This is a leadership challenge and opportunity.

Ira Chaleff has identified several ways this part of the softer side of leadership can be enhanced. He encourages leaders:

1) "Place people around you who will tell you what they see, not what they think you want to see;

2) "Present your ideas for change as propositions, not as impositions;

3) "Listen carefully [and] ask questions carefully, rewarding the questioner, creating a culture of question encouragement."[24]

Leader-followers also need to encourage organizational opportunity-finding, not just wrong-finding. People sometimes have a greater affinity for organizational wrong-finding than they do for right-finding, or looking for creative ways to approach challenging situations. Leaders need to ask questions, such as, "How can we make it better?" rather than asking only the proverbial "So what's wrong with it?" Again, these healthy practices are optimized when mutual trust is part of the organizational culture. In its absence, this kind of authentic sharing will likely not take place.

Various people from time to time have raised the question: What makes for a truly effective leader? One group of writers has answered this way: Effective leaders understand this leader-follower dynamic: "While the findings fill volumes, the consistent picture of the effective leader is one who adopts the style of a 'super-follower,' who serves with followers' blessing and consent, and who is able to inspire because [they are] first able to respond to their needs and concerns."[25]

This idea of a super-follower has strong grounding biblically, as those who seek the way of Jesus of Nazareth are first called to be

PUTTING THE IDEA TO WORK

Leaders who understand this lead-follow dynamic are unafraid of putting themselves in a position where their work can be challenged. This understanding can inform the kind of team leaders place around themselves. Those who require followers to always salute and stay quiet leave themselves vulnerable to blind spots, which can ultimately marginalize their leadership effectiveness.

Lead-follow leaders build accountability systems around their leadership, to ensure accountability to their followers.

Lead-follow leaders are unafraid to make decisions but usually seek input before those decisions are finalized. They gain the insights of followers through questions such as, "What did we miss?" and "How can we improve the decision?"

His followers. For those continuing to learn about what being a follower of Jesus means, especially within an organizational culture, implementing the idea of being a leader-follower in the organizations they serve and lead will not be a large step to take.

The reality, once again, is that leaders are often leading and following the same group at different times and in different ways. There is a time to lead and there is a time to follow. An effective leader has developed this soft skill of learning of when to do each.

CHAPTER 11

Understand That the Greatest Soft Skill Is Love

"He who loves not, lives not."

—Ramon Llull[1]

"The world thinks love is a scarcity to be guarded. Jesus knows it as an abundance to be shared."

—Skye Jethani[2]

"There is no greater love than to lay down one's life for one's friends."

—Jesus of Nazareth[3]

"The only prize worth winning is love. . . . I know with a terrible certainty that the only prize worth chasing [love] is the prize I've managed to lose."

—Susan Howatch, *Ultimate Prizes*[4]

Eugene Peterson, creator of *The Message* paraphrase of the Bible, begins his introductory note to 1st, 2nd, and 3rd John this way: "The two most difficult things to get straight in life are love and God. More often than not, the mess people make of their lives can be traced to failure or stupidity or meanness in one or both of

these areas."[5] Several millennia ago, the writer of the book of Exodus made this observation about God's leadership and the Israelites:
"The people you rescued were led by your powerful love."[6] Paul,
writing to the Corinthian church, talked with his readers about the
things not yet clearly seen, like "squinting in a fog, peering through
a mist." He notes that, eventually, that weather will clear up: "But
for right now, until that completeness, we have three things to do to
lead us. . . . Trust steadily in God, hope unswervingly, love extrava-
gantly. And the best of the three is love."[7]

On first reading, these words seem fully appropriate only for religious people and religious organizations. *Fast Company* magazine
may have changed that view with one of its cover stories, when it
boldly proclaimed, "Love Is the Killer App," subtitling the article,
"Why faith beats fear, greed isn't good, and nice guys finish first,
really." In the article, Tim Sanders, formerly chief solutions officer of
Yahoo, said, "I'm here to convince you that what the business world
needs now is love!"[8] Sanders defined what he meant by love, quot-
ing Milton Mayeroff, as "the selfless promotion of the growth of the
other." He notes that "when you help others grow to become the best
people they can be, you are being loving—and as a result, you grow."[9]

Sanders seems to be suggesting that when you give your life
away by investing in another, you find yourself growing as well. This
counterintuitive focus about embedding a culture of love within the
organization being led is yet another soft-skill focus that needs to be
embraced by leaders.

Ironically, Sanders' words initially come across as words that
often have no home in the business community. Not surprisingly,
they seem to align more with words that Jesus of Nazareth used in
the gospels. He repeatedly called His followers to love one another,
and to love God with all of their hearts, minds, and souls.

Some will rightly argue that organizations can't demonstrate
love, only people can. Of course. Organizations are technically only

pieces of paper, legal corporations, put together by people, including lawyers, organized to achieve some missional or business purpose. So long as an organization remains only a legal document, any discussion about love is moot. But eventually, organizations come to life. People with personalities and beliefs are hired; boards are put in place; priorities are established; budgets are developed; programs are created; products and material bought and sold, and people are served, which creates revenue and expense streams.

The people who work and serve at such places—with their accumulated commitments, skills, values, personalities, prejudices, strengths, and weaknesses—become the people who give personality to what otherwise would only be a legal entity. It is the sum total of the behaviors and attitudes, expressed through the employees and volunteers of an organization, that give it personality. An organization or corporation, just like a person, has an embedded personality or culture by which it is often known.

To illustrate: Often when people are searching for a church home and engaged in the church visitation process, they may come to the conclusion that the church was "very warm" or "very cold." They obviously were not talking about room temperature, but rather about the church's collective personality—at least as they experienced it. I've often experienced this as I have visited other organizations or college and university campuses. People visiting come away with clear impressions, positive or negative, seldom neutral, about the people and attitudes represented at a particular place. One of the amazing things we often heard from prospective student visitors and their families was that they just knew this was the place where they wanted to come to attend university. They wanted to be part of the amazing community of students, faculty, and staff. Clearly, leaders can impact an organization's personality and culture by leading with their authentic love of people and place.

There is probably no better source that evidences a definition of love than the life and teachings of Jesus of Nazareth. He talked incessantly about the importance of love, even calling us to love our enemies. He noted that in their contemporary culture, the usual practices were for people to hate their enemies and love their friends. In terms of people issues, our days are not so different. Yet, Jesus reminds us that the kind of behavior that pleases God is this: "But I tell you to love your enemies and pray for anyone who mistreats you. Then you will be acting like your Father in heaven. . . . If you love only those people who love you, will God reward you for that?"[10] Kierkegaard calls this kind of "backward" teaching an example of an inverse dialectic—that is, thinking in an opposite way from what normally one would think to be the case. In the Scriptures, love has that quality.[11]

Jesus continues in John 15:12: "Now I tell you to love each other as I have loved you." The apostle John discusses this important point in several places in the Bible, such as in 1 John 4:7a: "My dear friends, we must love each other. Love comes from God, and when we love each other, it shows that we have been given new life." Paul, in Romans 12:10, called us to "Love each other as brothers and sisters and honor others more than you do yourself."

The Scriptures talk about love in dozens of passages that make striking claims. For instance, Jesus profoundly notes that outside people will validate that His mission was from the Father when those outsiders witness the love that exists among His followers.[12] Paradoxically, the inference is that by not exhibiting that kind of love, followers of Jesus would be invalidating His mission as the God-sent one. When people hold a grudge, or refuse to talk to or refuse to forgive one another, they are making a telling mark for others about Jesus' message, but certainly not in a positive direction.

What, then, might the face of love look like in the context of organizational culture?

The Look of Love in Organizational Culture

To many people, the word "love" tends to be one of those soft, "touchy-feely" words. The secular culture doesn't help with its multiple meanings of love. For example, one definition goes in the direction of sexual passion and desire. Another goes in the direction of having "a profoundly, tender, passionate, affection for another person." Still another talks about "warm personal attachment or deep affection."

The Bible tends to be very precise in its use of the word love, using three different definitions.[13] One definition is to talk about love in a sexual or erotic way—love as *eros*. A good example of this kind of love can be found in the Song of Solomon in the Bible. This is not the meaning of love as used in this chapter. The second way love is defined is in describing the love between a husband and wife in a healthy marriage, a fervent love for another person—love as *phileo*. Again, this is love expressed to another in helpful kinds of ways. The third way love is referenced is where one loves another so much that he would be willing to give up his life for the one loved. This is truly unconditional love, love of another no matter what. This kind of love characterizes God's love for humankind—love as *agape*.

Many of us have heard of or experienced stories of people doing extraordinary things to save the life or to improve the life of another. One example in my life was my brother-in-law, unmarried and just drafted into the army. Upon hearing that his younger brother, just married, was being sent by the Marines to Vietnam, he volunteered to take his place and go to Vietnam. While unsuccessful, his act represented an example of giving another a gift of love. Sometimes persons give up healthy organs, even at the risk of their own health, so that another might enjoy a much higher quality of life. When I talk about love in the organizational setting, the kind of love I have in mind is represented by the *phileo* and *agape* definitions of love, these second and third definitions of the word love.

THE CHAPTER IDEA

Effective leaders champion the impact of the power of love within their organization—not as some nebulous concept but as a foundational and relational necessity.

Organizations have personalities, which represent the sum total of the behaviors and attitudes expressed through an organization's colleagues and volunteers.

Organizations can demonstrate a culture of love through how they care for their people—and how those persons communicate that love by serving each other, and others beyond the organization. Love means sharing everything, without any expectation of return, because "it's the right thing to do." Jesus of Nazareth is the example of what love looks like, both inside and outside of an organization.

Organizational Love Means a Commitment to Growing People.

I've already referenced Sanders' initial answer: "Love means a commitment to growing people, selflessly, whether or not the person you report to has the same commitment to you." Our commitment to growing people needs to be selfless and unconditional. If I only ask, "So, what's in it for the organization?" I have already moved away from being selfless to being selfish. A commitment to growing people based on love means we're committed to doing so because of the benefit to them, and because we know there will be a resulting benefit to the organization. Leaders realize that investing in their people sometimes creates new opportunities for the employee helped, and sometimes they take a different job elsewhere as a result. But leaders invest anyhow, simply because it is the right thing to do. This is the kind of action the apostle Paul had in mind when he called us to "honor others more than you do yourself."

Leaders need to view people at the places they serve as a trust that they are called to steward. Those people have gifts and abilities that can be developed, not only better to serve the organization, but also better to serve God's broader purposes and the common good. This commitment to growing people for their own sake, not just for the organization, is a critical element of demonstrating organizational love.

Once on a campus walk, I met one staff member who had just completed his doctorate, two more who were almost finished, and another just getting started. Still another was just returning from a professional development program. Several more were either just returning from sabbaticals or headed in that direction. All were excited and grateful for these experiences. Professional growth programs such as these supported by the university were ways love could be expressed organizationally. The good news is that these types of programs also added to the quality of contribution the employee gave back to the university. It made the people who were part of them feel good, both about themselves and about their contribution to the university.

One of the quotes that Maya Angelou is known for is: "I've learned that people will forget what you said, people will forget what you did, but people will never forget how you made them feel."[14] Loving people by growing people helps them feel good about themselves and also about the places where they work.

An important question for leaders, then, is this: "Am I adding value to the people in this organization, and can I do this better?" Whenever a person entered retirement from organizations where I had served as president, I always enjoyed hearing him or her recite the various ways he or she had helped the organization grow. But if that is all I heard, then I was disappointed. I also wanted to hear them say how much they had grown because of the organization's commitment to their personal and professional growth. That ought to be a clear goal for a leader, and one of the ways love can be expressed in the organization. Investing in people, of course, can be done in multiple ways with multiple strategies.

Organizational Love Means Sharing Everything

Sanders doesn't stop there. He insists that organizational love needs to be more than just talk and that action needs to be part of the discussion. In his second answer to the question, "What does the face of organizational love look like?" he suggests it is this: "Share everything, plain and simple." His view of love ultimately calls for the sharing of everything we know: "your knowledge, networks, and compassion with your business partners." Then almost Jesus-like, he challenges his readers to do this willingly, without any expectation of return: "Behave this way not because you expect something in return—a *quid pro quo*—but because it is the right way to behave. The less you expect in return for acts of professional generosity, the more you will receive."[15]

Jesus instructed His followers to give their lives away, noting that if people wanted to find their lives they had to be willing to lose them; or if people wanted to be first, they had to learn to be last. Jesus told people they would increase in God's eyes only by learning to decrease.

It is hard to imagine words such as these coming from an executive of a major technology company. Most likely we might expect it from pastors of megachurches, heads of major Christian nonprofits, or even presidents of Christian universities. Unfortunately, many of us are busy building our own empires, our own platforms, or adding value to our brand in order to gain market share or some kind of competitive advantage over one another. Many are unaware that comparison and competition bring out the beast in us, not the best in us. As Dr. David Allen puts it, comparison and competition fuel our hurt trails.[16]

Pastors sometime complain about "sheep stealing"—that is, when they lose members to another church's more aggressive programming. Christian college and university presidents might complain about the ideas, programs, and students a competitor stole or bought. Other nonprofits might complain about a competitor stealing "our" donors, or getting the large monetary gift that "we" should have gotten. Each of these attitudes flies in the face of what Jesus taught. Indeed, if the kingdom is being advanced, and if we say that's part of our organizational commitment, why does it matter who planted, who watered, who cultivated, or who harvested (1 Cor. 3:5–9)? Isn't it God who brings the increase, and isn't it for His purposes and kingdom that we use our gifts anyway?

When Sanders advises us to "share everything," that advice flies in the face of many who have spent their lifetimes accumulating degrees or money, developing creative ideas, and pursuing intellectual property. Is it because we're selfish? Is it because we want the praise and the money rather than someone else? Is it because we want to be recognized as the leader who brought major change and accomplishment to leadership, not another? Many of us would not think of sharing our trade secrets with other competitors, or our copyrighted materials with others. Yet, this is what Sanders suggests and seems to be what Jesus commands.

Just maybe, Sanders is onto something here. What if competing denominational church leaders, in the professed name of love for Jesus of Nazareth and the advancement of His kingdom, annually got together and shared all of their plans for the next year with each other, so duplication and waste might be avoided and strategic kingdom impact enhanced? Not some of their plans, but all of them? What if Christian university presidents did the same thing? What about Christian publishers? What about Bible agencies and those who hold copyrighted material to Scripture and music-related products? What is gained or lost by our not doing that, in terms of kingdom gain or loss? Perhaps we ought to be asking why leaders are not doing that now. Might that be a worthy goal for the leaders of the next generation who are committed to pursuing the soft skill of organizational love?

Fortunately, there are growing examples where this is happening, like with the International Sports Coalition, which gives everything away for free, even their intellectual property. The agencies involved in Bible translation and Scripture distribution are also cooperating in new ways regarding their intellectual property, through apps such as YouVersion. Natural disasters such as massive flooding and hurricanes also bring out the best in competitors, who upon seeing the greater need of the hurting sometimes work together, even serving competitor's clients, because they know it is the right thing to do.

When I worked in New York City, I had many opportunities to test this "give it away" mindset. One of our major donor foundations, for example, insisted that cooperation and collaboration were conditions for receipt of an eight-figure gift. One of the conditions was that organizations being assisted needed to set aside their individual goals and agendas, and instead work together, each contributing their necessary expertise to achieve the overall collective needs within a particular part of the world. This "work together, give-it-away mindset," while rare, was a great success. On the other hand, I remember inviting one major ministry to gather together with many others of us to coordinate our work in given countries, in order to avoid waste and duplication. Unfortunately, that invitation was refused because that agency only wanted to do its own thing, certain that God had blessed their efforts because they had not cooperated with others.

Universities have all kinds of opportunities to "give it away." A relatively recent initiative has been the development of "Massive

Open Online Courses" (MOOCS) that are given away for free. The eventual hope, though, is to monetize these efforts in some way. Other colleges and universities, and nonprofits, are pursuing collaborative "back-end" service opportunities, such as pooled insurance services, utilities, and joint purchasing. What Sanders has in mind may go beyond these simple but appropriate initiatives. Sanders wants "no expectation of a return," and many of the examples I have used thus far have an expectation of a return—mainly, a reduction in operating costs.

Here's an example that doesn't: Among other areas of distinction, Taylor University has a national reputation for the quality of its student development programs. It has been viewed by others as one of the national leaders in this area. This program provides a kind of "secret sauce" for the integrated Taylor experience. Around 2012, Taylor began a unique graduate program, a master's degree in higher education (MAHE). I was enthusiastically supportive of going forward with this because of the quality we could deliver to students. But here was the rub: By going forward with this program, and having multiple other universities now hiring that program's graduates, we were in essence giving away our "secret sauce" to others. This is precisely the kind of action that Sanders is calling forth in leaders to share everything.

These examples illustrate the difficulty of pursuing this "give it away" strategy. But in a very small way it also illustrates the potential, if not the imperative, of sharing everything. We must fight our tendencies to hoard, rather than to give away; to collaborate with others rather than to separate our efforts, keeping them in isolation from others. Evidence of our understanding of this key soft skill for leaders is both to ask and answer the question, "What can I share, and what am I already sharing that would benefit others, including my competitors? What more can I be doing?" Usually we're not wired to think this way, let alone to act upon it.

PUTTING THE IDEA TO WORK

Love in action means a commitment to growing people and never letting them settle for "good enough" when they're capable of excellence.

When love marks an organizational culture, its people ask questions like: "What can I share with others for their benefit—even with my competitors?"

Leaders immersed in a culture of love practice this wise counsel: "Healthy community is not the absence of conflict or brokenness or messiness, but the presence of Jesus in the middle of it."

Organizational leaders, when necessary and appropriate, willingly give up their leadership position for the greater benefit of the organizational mission, because they know that leadership is never solely about them.

Organizational Love Means Loving People—Even When It Gets Messy

There is more to this idea of organizational love. In the words of Jesus and the apostle Paul, we see several additional meanings of what love in an organizational context looks like: "Love means a commitment to love both one's enemies and also to those who have extended mistreatment." This means leaders need to show love to their critics and naysayers, not just those who affirm their leadership.

This means not striking back or retaliating against those who have mistreated us, or who otherwise did something "worthy" of our assigning the label "enemy." This biblical teaching has both a personal and an organizational dimension—and often, it gets messy. One of our Taylor alumni, J. R. Briggs, spoke at one of our chapels and made this interesting comment about the messiness of organizational community, calling it a mess worth making: "Healthy community is not the absence of conflict or brokenness or messiness but the presence of Jesus in the middle of it all."

In the context of church, Eugene Peterson, in his introductory notes to the book of James, draws an interesting analogy between a hospital, whose job it is to care for the sick, and the church: "Just as a hospital collects the sick under one roof and labels them as such, the church collects sinners. Many of the people outside the hospital are every bit as sick as the ones inside, but their illnesses are either undiagnosed or disguised. It's similar with sinners outside the church. So Christian churches are not, as a rule, model communities of good behavior. They are rather, places where human misbehavior is brought out in the open, faced, and dealt with."[17]

At Taylor University we introduced a practice that illustrates Peterson's point. Acknowledging the reality of the messiness within our intentional community, we have annually distributed towels with the words "one another" embroidered on them, in the spirit of Jesus' example in John 13, where he washed his disciples' feet. These towels were tangible reminders to us to live fully committed to each other, as well as to the "one anothers" of Scripture, such as to encourage one another, exhort one another, bear one another's burdens, and of course, love one another. It was an emotional experience to be given one of these towels by our student leaders, and I placed it in a prominent place in my office. It is a daily reminder that I was and still am called to love people, no matter what, as I embrace the life of a servant leader. In doing so, I choose to mark my life with love.

In any organization there are usually multiple examples of people who believe, rightly or wrongly, that they have been mistreated. Those who feel mistreated sometimes strike out, often causing great personal harm and hurt to those responsible for their pain. It has been observed that often "*hurt* people, hurt *people*." At the same time, sometimes people who feel mistreated project an attitude of elitism, believing they are above ever causing an offense to anyone. It is always the fault of the other, never their fault. No matter. Jesus' teaching to all, leaders included, is not to strike back—even when one is perhaps justified in doing so. Instead, he calls us to be peacemakers.

There is also an interorganizational aspect to this issue. Often institutions, businesses, even churches, do things that could hurt their competitors or neighbors around the corner, as they pursue their organization's agenda. In the higher education world, for example, it is not uncommon for a university—sometimes located hundreds of miles away—to set up shop close to or adjacent to a university already offering a similar program. Why not collaborate and cooperate instead? Why the need always, always to have to do your own thing?

Comparison and competition often bring out the beast in us. Love puts a stop to that and requires, instead, the taking of the high road—even backing away from a planned initiative if it harms a competitor. Even when wronged by a competitor, the proper response is to show the face of love.

One high-road leadership practice we tried to follow was to never to tear down a competitor, even when an opportunity to do so might have been warranted. Rather, the words of Philippians 4:8 are timeless and have application at both the personal and organizational level: "[F]ix your thoughts on what is true, and honorable, and right, and pure, and lovely, and admirable. Think about things that are excellent and worthy of praise." Every person and every competitor has these kinds of attributes. The organizational face of love remembers them. And every leader champions them, knowing that "love covers a multitude of sins."

The Greatest Soft Skill Is Love

One of the most powerful chapters in the Bible about love is 1 Corinthians 13, and it represents a fourth face of love: "Love is kind and patient, never jealous, boastful, proud, or rude. Love isn't selfish or quick-tempered. It doesn't keep a record of wrongs that others do. Love rejoices in the truth, but not in evil. Love is always supportive, loyal, hopeful, and trusting. Love never fails. . . . But now there are faith, hope, and love. But of these three, the greatest is love."[18]

Regrettably, these verses are usually relegated to weddings and heard by many as love poems, as our next-door neighbor in New York City once described it to Marylou. We know that these words represent the way God loves us. But can we courageously aspire to trying to love each other in a similar way? These teachings have relevance, again, to both the personal and family life as well as to the organization. It would be quickly evident just what the organizational impact would be if every employee, including leaders, consistently modeled kindness and patience in relationships. The positive impact on organizational culture would be profound if people were seldom or rarely boastful, rude, jealous, or prideful. What would it look like to have leaders who would not be selfish or quick-tempered, but instead, balanced and even-tempered? What impact would those examples have on staff members who were encouraged to "go and do likewise"?

I am amazed as to how this happened repeatedly on our campus. For example, one of our colleagues was in the process of losing his young son, who had a degenerative disease and was slowly slipping toward death. He and his wife, who at the same time had two parents in hospice care, had no funds to cover the burial expenses of their young son. So the department where he worked, unbeknown to him, took up a collection to cover those expenses and presented the funds to him in a surprise meeting. The gift was received with great gratitude and with many tears. That's what love looks like in an organization.

Jesus of Nazareth in our best example of what love looks like. As the Son of God, representative of God in a human form, He was willing to give His life for us—even though we didn't deserve it, even when we failed to understand our need for His love. When asked, "Of all the ways you as God could answer, I need to know one thing: What is the law's most important commandment?" Without hesitation, Jesus responded this way in Matthew 22:37–40: "You must love the Lord your God with all your heart, all your soul, and all your mind. This is the first and greatest commandment. A second one is equally important. Love your neighbor as yourself. The entire law and all the demands of the prophets are based upon these two commandments."

Loving God, and loving people, expressed in multiple ways and nuanced across multiple cultures is what love looks like. Again, in the organizational context, growing people, sharing everything, loving people even when it gets messy—are merely illustrative responses to the question, "What does love look like in the organization?"

What, then, are likely to be the results of pursuing this kind of an organizational vision of love? Softness in decisions? Disgruntled staff? Hardly. Sanders' discovery was "that the business people who are the busiest, the happiest, and the most prosperous are the ones who are also the most generous with their knowledge and their expertise." It is the people who learned to genuinely love, not the "barracudas, sharks, and piranhas,"[19] who made the difference. Author Laurie Kaplan Singh builds on this point, writing about "CEOs Under Scrutiny," noting that "most management failures can be attributed to arrogance or stupidity—and it is a contest for which is worse. As a result, analysts are increasingly scrutinizing the soft side as well as the hard side of a CEO's personality."[20] And this soft side includes the leader's ability to practice love within the organization.

When we reflect on the businesses and organizations that do it right—that make common-sense decisions in the best interest of others, not just the company—one of the best financial performers in the airline industry, Southwest Airlines, comes to mind. The paradox is that by showing love, kindness, care, and respect for its passengers, the company reaps substantial financial benefits to its bottom line. In the university world, when that happens, dramatically improved student retention and employee longevity result.

If this is true, then why is love in the organizational context not pursued, and in fact usually ignored? Often the reason is because we ultimately do not believe it will work; it doesn't seem practical. We read, for example, the words of Jesus, "give your life away," but we believe that if we do that, we'll ultimately be the loser. We acknowledge His words, "if you lose your life, you'll find it," but perceive those words to be downright unworkable. We not only don't want to lose our organizational lives, we want to hang on to our leadership positions even tighter. As a result, pursuing and developing this culture of love is viewed as simply impractical, if not downright impossible to achieve—so why waste the energy trying?

The paradox is that those who cling to their leadership positions—those who want to hold tightly to their leadership role, no matter what—run the risk of making the worst decisions, because their operating plumb line for decisions is not "What is best for this organization, or will best serve the mission?" but rather, "What will likely let me continue in my leadership role?" The tough decisions are deferred, "kicking the proverbial can [or difficult organizational issues] down the road."

Leaders who understand and are committed to embedding love as a soft skill into their organizational culture are not afraid of losing whatever leadership position they have been given. They understand that their position doesn't belong to them for private purposes or for personal gain in the first place. Rather, it has been given as a trust to be exercised of behalf of others and for a larger mission and purpose. When leaders understand that, they understand the true genius of giving themselves away, and that truly the greatest soft skill is love.

Conclusion

◆ We have discussed just some of the soft skills, behaviors, practices, and attitudes that can be deployed every day in homes and workplaces. The leadership challenge is for leaders to not only recognize the importance of these types of soft skills in their leadership, but also to take steps to enhance their further development in these skills through practice. Again, it is not that hard skills are unnecessary in the home or workplace. Rather, it is that by themselves, hard skills are inadequate as leadership capacities to meet and sustain the comprehensive demands and needs of people and the places where they work and serve.

I am often asked this question: "So, where should I start in the development of soft skills?" The practical answer is that it probably doesn't matter much because soft skills are interrelated and interconnected in multiple ways. Growth and development in one soft skill area will likely spill over and influence others, giving lift in multiple ways. Take, for instance, developing the soft skill of fitness renewal. As a leader's fitness improves, there will be trickle-down benefits: Leaders will feel better about themselves; they will likely have more energy and improved focus; and they will no doubt be able to work smarter and with a greater sense of purpose. Those benefits will also likely enhance personal, family, and organizational impact.

Alternately, and for persons of faith, there may be a better answer to the question, "Where does one start?" The former president and CEO of Compassion International, Wess Stafford, notes the importance of beginning by building one's spiritual foundation and providing for sacred space: "[Leaders] are in a spiritual battle, so walk closely with God. Listen to His whisper. I begin each day, no matter where I am, no matter how busy I am, with an hour of listening and prayer."[1] That sounds an awful lot like establishing the need for sacred space and building one's spiritual foundation as priorities. In effect, it means taking the time and making the space that will allow the leader/instrument to be in tune before the concert, not after it has been performed. It surely will improve the probability of success, however defined.

As I referenced earlier, during one stretch of my leadership journey, when both the marriage ride and the leadership assignment were a bit bumpy, Marylou and I made a scheduled appointment with our marriage coach for a couple of sessions to help us get back on track. After a few hours, he said something like this: "Gene, so what do you want?" The lawyer in me took over the conversation, and I retorted something like: "With regard to what?" I'll not forget his response: "You go figure it out. And don't discuss it with Marylou. Write it down and come back and we'll talk tomorrow." So, what did I want? What was important in my life as I was then living it? What did I want to be important going forward? Facing that question and struggling with its answer provided a breakthrough insight that pointed my life in a better direction.

Unfortunately, many people in leadership roles have not really faced that question: "So what do you want?" with regard to developing soft skills, personally or in the workplace. We think, "I know I should be doing a better job of loving my family. I know I should be living my life in the workplace in a way so that the people where I work feel loved and appreciated." But as is often the case, leaders never quite get around to much of the soft stuff because the hard stuff simply dominates and overpowers the organizational agenda. As a result, the organization loses; so, too, do its people; so, too, does the leader and all families involved.

One writer who understands this soft-skill challenge and who has written about this question is Harvard Business School professor Clayton Christensen. His question is not, "So what do you want?" It is a similar question of, "So how will you measure your life?"[2] His question is the kind of question leaders need to ask of themselves and others. Christensen believes a good answer to that question involves consideration of five strategies:

1) developing an approach for how you will live your life;

2) figuring out how to allocate your resources, all of them and however defined;

3) creating a culture that in almost intuitive ways gives guidance through the difficult times;

4) living life with integrity—what he calls avoiding the "marginal costs" such as, "I'll only cheat this one time," and;

5) making a lifelong commitment to living a life of humility—making sure it's not only about you.

Interestingly, none of these strategies involve hard skills. Rather, they are all about what I've been calling the softer side of leadership. And interestingly, each of the soft skills discussed throughout this book fits somewhere within the five components or strategies Christensen identifies. For instance, developing a strategy for your life includes the focus of chapter 1, making sure that as leaders we celebrate sacred space and allow time for deep thinking. Setting the kinds of spiritual foundations discussed in chapter 2, and fitness renewal discussed in chapter 5, are all parts of developing a strategy for our lives.

With regard to allocation of resources, that kind of investment should come in many ways. In particular, the focus on self-discovery learning in multiple places in our lives is an important place for continual resource investment. There are several chapters dealing with what Christensen calls creating a culture. Some important elements of putting a culture in place include celebrating the importance of creativity (chapter 6), building trust (chapter 7) and recognizing the importance of forgiveness (chapter 9). All are necessary parts of an organization's culture. The chapter on accountability, chapter 8, emphasizes one of the most important ways to live a life of integrity—mutual accountability. That leads to positive results both in the home and in the workplace. Without it, leaders are in trouble or at least headed for it.

So, how can humility, Christensen's fifth strategy, be made an integral part of how organizations function? It comes down to key elements of staying connected to their own hearts, as well as to the hearts of their people (chapter 4); understanding the importance of love (chapter 11); and understanding and mediating the tension between the leading and the following roles practiced by leaders (chapter 10). Whether you use the framework referenced by Christensen or some other framework, the message is simple: The softer side of leadership, represented by the use of soft skills, needs to be an important part of every leader's portfolio. Soft skills play incredibly important roles within families, within organizations, and within cultures.

I saw an example of soft skills at work culturally during a trip in South Korea, particularly the soft skill of accountability. My wife Marylou and I were leaving the train station in Seoul to take the high-speed train to Pusan. As we waited to board, one of my Korean colleagues came running up to me and asked, "Did you see that yellow line back there on the platform?" Of course I had missed it. He went on to explain that the Koreans call that line an ethical line. What they mean is that since tickets are not asked to be shown for passage on this train ride, because of high honor and trust, people who don't have tickets should not proceed past that yellow line—the ethical line, a line that implicitly serves as an external decision point regarding trust and honor. But there is no external enforcement.

People adhere to this expectation because of their commitment to living their lives with integrity. They do it because they want to, not because of some kind of external "have to" regulation. I assume there are people who cross that ethical line without a ticket, but I doubt that they are Korean.

At the beginning of this book, I noted that effective leaders embrace hard skills, but not hard skills alone. Effective leaders also embrace and develop soft skills. It is that combination, hard and soft, implemented and integrated together, that results in more effective leadership and enhanced organizational capacity. Dewhurst and Willmalt illustrate this when referencing the hard skill of technology: "No computer will ever manage by walking around. . . . We're firmly convinced that simultaneous growth in the importance of softer management skills **and** [emphasis added] technology [a hard skill] will boost the complexity and richness of the senior-executive role."[3] Why? Because "Today's CEOs sit in a world of nuances that require judgment, insight, and *the ability to weigh in on the soft issues—not just the hard ones*" (emphasis added).[4]

The softer side of leadership is not just a catchy phrase or a collection of catchy words. Rather, paying more attention to soft skills, along with hard ones, identifies a type of roadmap, a way forward, for facing and addressing the complex issues and opportunities that await the next generation of leaders. Hard and soft skills together enable leaders to lead more effectively, doing "all the good they can, by all the means they can, in all the ways they can, in all the places they can, to all the people they can, as long as they can," for their families, for the organizations they serve, and for the glory of God![5]

ENDNOTES

Introduction

1. Michael Grothaus, "How to Become an Engineer with People Skills," *Fast Company*, April 2, 2014, https://www.fastcompany.com/3028585/a-practical-guide-to-becoming-a-whole-developer.
2. Investopedia, "Hard Skills," May 15, 2010, http://www.investopedia.com/terms/h/hard-skills.asp (accessed April 2014).
3. Goleman, Daniel. "The Emotional Intelligence Skills Employers Want Now," *The Career Development Center Blog*, July 8, 2013, http://blogs.oregonstate.edu/careerservices/2012/11/30/emotional-intelligence-what-is-it-and-why-do-employers-want-emotionally-intelligent-employees.
4. Amy J. C. Cuddy, Matthew Kohut, John Neffinger, "Connect, Then Lead," *HarvardBusiness Review* (July/August 2013): 56.
5. "Soft Skills," *slideplayer.com*, http://slideplayer.com/slide/9696417.
6. "Soft skills," *Wikipedia*, https://en.m.wikipedia.org/wiki/Soft_skills.
7. Steve Leybourne, "Project Mangers Competencies: Soft Skills Are the Hard Part!" http://www.projectmanagementinpractice.com/wp-content/uploads/2015/02/Leybourne-Soft-Skill-Competencies.pdf.
8. Dominic Barton and Mei Ye, "Developing China's business leaders: A conversation with Yingyi Qian," McKinsley Quarterly (July 2013), http://www.mckinsey.com/global-themes/leadership/developing-chinas-business-leaders.

9. Matthew 23:10 (CEV).
10. Barbara Kellerman, "Required Reading," *Harvard Business Review* 79 (December 2001):15–24.
11. Rich Karlgaard, "Good Guy, Tough Spot," *Forbes*, October 29, 2001, 47.
12. Kellerman, "Required Reading."
13. Michael Grothaus, "How to Become an Engineer with People Skills."
14. Tim Sanders, "Love Is the Killer App," *Fast Company*, January 31, 2002, https://www.fastcompany.com/44541/love-killer-app.
15. Catherine Fredman, "Hal Rosenbluth, MBA Mythbuster," *Chief Executive*, February 1, 2002, https://chiefexecutive.net/hal-rosenbluth-mba-mythbuster__trashed.
16. Cuddy, et al., "Connect, Then Lead," 57.
17. See also Eugene B. Habecker, *The Other Side of Leadership* (Wheaton, IL: Victor Books, 1987); *Leading with a Follower's Heart* (Wheaton, IL: Victor Books, 1990), and *Rediscovering the Soul of Leadership* (Wheaton, IL: Victor Books, 1996).

Chapter 1—Protect Sacred Space and Enable Deep Thinking

1. Psalm 24:1.
2. "Sacred Space," Minnesota Episcopal Environmental Stewardship Commission, www.env-steward.com/reflect/space.htm.
3. Todd Henry, *The Accidental Creative* (New York: Penguin Press, 2011), 16.
4. Todd Henry, "Defining Your Sacred Space," *Accidental Creative*, www.accidentalcreative.com/inspiration/defining-your-sacred-space.
5. Stephen R. Covey, *First Things First* (New York: Simon and Schuster, 1994), as quoted in Habecker, *Rediscovering the Soul of Leadership*, 9.

6. Frances Hesselbein, quoted in *Chief Executive*, January/February, 1995, 38.
7. Psalm 121:1.
8. Psalm 46:10.
9. Isaiah 30:15b.
10. Exodus 33:15.
11. "What Happened to Downtime? The Extinction of Deep Thinking and Sacred Space," *Fast Company*, November 5, 2010, 1, www.FastCompany.com/node/1700298.
12. See Anne Morrow Lindbergh, *Gift from the Sea* (New York: Pantheon Books, 1955).
13. Henri J. M. Nouwen, *The Return of the Prodigal Son* (New York: Doubleday, 1992), 17.
14. "What Happened to Downtime?" op. cit, 2.
15. See *APU Life*, 27:2 (Summer 2014), 18.
16. William Deresiewicz, "Solitude and Leadership," *American Scholar*, March 1, 2010, theamericanscholar.org/solitude-and-leadership.
17. Henry Cloud, *Necessary Endings* (New York: Harper Collins, 2010).
18. Deresiewicz, op. cit., 6.
19. Ibid.
20. Ibid., 7.
21. Ibid., 9. See also Uri Friedman, "David Brooks' 5-Step Guide to Being Deep," *The Atlantic*, July 1, 2014, www.theatlantic.com/national/archive/2014/07david-brooks-5-step-guide-to-being-deep/373699.
22. Henri Nouwen, *The Wounded Healer* (Garden City, NY: Image Books, 1979), 90.
23. Deresiewicz, op. cit.
24. Genesis 2:1–3.
25. Exodus 20:8–10a.

26. Exodus 23:12b.
27. Leviticus 23:3a.
28. Mark 2:27.
29. Skye Jethani, "Making Music of Our Work," *skyejethani.com*, August 13, 2016.

Chapter 2—Build a Foundation for Leadership

1. Luke 6:48–49.
2. Proverbs 24:10.
3. Stephen R. Covey, *First Things First* (New York: Simon and Schuster, 1996).
4. Ibid, 88–89.
5. Ibid, 89.
6. 2 Peter 1:5–7.
7. 2 Timothy 3:16–17.
8. M. Neil Browne and Stuart M. Keeley, *Asking the Right Questions*, 11th Edition (London: Pearson, 2014).
9. John C. Maxwell, *Good Leaders Ask Great Questions* (New York: Center Street, 2014).
10. Patrick Lencioni, "The Unsexy Power of Discipline," *The Hub*, September 2017, https://tablegroup.com/hub/post/the-unsexy-power-of-discipline.
11. Evangelical Council on Financial Accountability (ECFA), "Focus on Accountability Quarterly Newsletter," Second Quarter 2014.
12. Ibid.
13. Skye Jethani, "Questions Are the Answer," *skyejethani.com*, June 2014. See also Noah Toly, "Asking the Right Questions," *Books and Culture*, November/December 2015, 14–15.
14. See Luke 21.
15. Story shared in an interview with Harold Myra, former President of Christianity Today, Inc., Taylor University, April 2014.
16. Lisa Lai, "Being a Strategic Leader Is about Asking the Right

Questions," *Harvard Business Review*, January 18, 2017, https://
hbr.org/2017/01/being-a-strategic-leader-is-about-asking-the-
right-questions.

17. Ibid.

18. Shared by Dr. Mark Labberton, President, Fuller Seminary, in a
devotional presented to the Taylor University Board of Trustees,
February 2014.

19. Daniel 3:18–19.

20. See *Life Essentials Study Bible* (Nashville: Holman Bible Publishers, 2011), 986.

21. Ibid., 983.

22. Ecclesiastes 7:8.

Chapter 3—Welcome Self-Discovery Learning

1. Henry Ford, "Quotable Quote," *goodreads.com*, https://www.
goodreads.com/quotes/37961-anyone-who-stops-learning-is-old-
whether-at-twenty-or.

2. Mary Louise Rowand, former trustee of the American Bible
Society, shared this with the author, c. 1992.

3. Eric Hoffer, "Quotable Quote," *goodreads.com*, https://www.
goodreads.com/quotes/10562-in-times-of-change-learners-
inherit-the-earth-while-the.

4. David Lidsky, "Satya Nadella Rewrites Microsoft's Code," *Fast
Company*, September 18, 2017, https://emailingnewsletter.com/
marketing-satya-nadella-rewrites-microsoft-s-code.html#.

5. Sirach 51:17, 23–26 (GNT).

6. Psalm 119:32 (CEV).

7. Proverbs 9:9b (CEV).

8. Proverbs 10:14a (CEV).

9. See Sanders, "Love is the Killer App," op. cit.

10. Noel Tichy, "Personal Histories," *Harvard Business Review*,
December 2001, 38.

11. Richard Chait, "Why Shouldn't Harvard's President Ask Tough Questions?" *Chronicle of Higher Education*, February 1, 2002, B20.

12. Gervase R. Bushe, *Clear Leadership* (Palo Alto, CA: Davies-Black Publishing, 2001), 40.

13. Ibid.

14. See Matthew 22:37–40 (CEV).

15. "Sight & Sound Theatres," *Wikipedia*, https://en.m.wikipedia.org/wiki/Sight_%26_Sound_Theatres The presentation referenced was seen in the Branson location, September 2017.

16. See Frederick Buechner, *Telling Secrets* (New York: Harper Collins, 1991).

17. Tichy, "Personal Histories," 29.

18. Ibid.

19. Ibid., 36.

20. Robert Reich, *The Future of Success* (New York: Alfred A. Knopf, 2001), 224.

21. C. J. Prince, "CEOs Anonymous," *Chief Executive*, March 2002, 33.

22. Henri Nouwen, *Inner Voice of Love* (New York: Doubleday, 1999), xiv–xv, xvii.

23. Henri Nouwen, *Reaching Out* (New York: Doubleday, 1975), 74.

24. Ibid., 74–75.

25. See the multiple writings of Danish philosopher Soren Kierkegaard.

26. Don and Susie Van Ryn, Colleen Newell, and Whitney Cerak, *Mistaken Identity* (New York: Howard Books, 2009).

27. James Oliver, "Still Not Happy?" *Business Life*, May 2001, 38.

28. Ken Gire, *Windows of the Soul* (Grand Rapids, MI: Zondervan, 1996), 49.

29. Bushe, *Clear Leadership*, 25.

30. Nouwen, *Reaching Out*, 40–41.

31. John Maxwell, *The 21 Indispensable Qualities of a Leader*

(Nashville: Thomas Nelson, 1999), xi.

32. Nouwen, *The Inner Voice of Love*, 86–87.

33. Stephen R. Covey, *Seven Habits of Highly Effective People* (New York: Simon & Schuster, 1989), 60–61.

34. See Covey, *SourcesofInsight.com*, July 25, 2012.

Chapter 4—Stay Connected to the Heart

1. Rainer Maria Rilke, "Quotable Quote," *goodreads.com*, https://www.goodreads.com/quotes/377482-the-work-of-the-eyes-is-done-go-now-and.

2. L. Frank Baum, *The Wonderful Wizard of Oz*, "Chapter 2: The Council with the Munchkins," http://kancoll.org/books/baum/oz05.htm.

3. Skye Jethani, "Psalm 1: Knowledge & Affection, *skyejethani.com*, http://skyejethani.com/devotional/psalm1.

4. Proverbs 4:23.

5. Frances Hesselbein, *Hesselbein on Leadership* (New York: Jossey-Bass, 2012), introduction.

6. Jeffrey J. Fox, *How to Become CEO* (New York: Hyperion, 1998), 1–3.

7. Frederick Buechner, *The Hungering Dark* (New York: Harper Collins, 1969), 32.

8. Reich, *The Future of Success*, 6.

9. Louis Patler, *Trendsmart* (Naperville, IL: Sourcebooks Inc., 2003), 245.

10. "Citizen Kraemer," *Chief Executive*, February 1, 2002.

11. David F. Allen, *In Search of the Heart* (Thomas Nelson, 1993).

12. Brent Curtis and John Eldredge, *Sacred Romance* (Thomas Nelson, 1997).

13. John Eldredge, *Wild at Heart* (Thomas Nelson, 2001).

14. Fenelon, *The Seeking Heart* (Gardiner, ME: Christian Books

Publishing House, 1992).

15. Allen, op. cit., 8.
16. Curtis and Eldredge, op. cit., 8–9.
17. Ibid., 2–3.
18. Ibid., 3.
19. Ibid.
20. In Peter J. Smith, ed., *Onward! 25 Years of Advice, Exhortation, and Inspiration from America's Best Commencement Speeches* (New York: Scribner, 2000), 38.
21. Nouwen, *Reaching Out*, 57–58.
22. Curtis and Eldredge, op. cit., 4–5.
23. John Eldredge, *Desire* (Nashville: Thomas Nelson, 2000), 8.
24. Fenelon, op. cit., 14.
25. Ibid., 96.
26. Ibid., 110.
27. Job 36:15 (CEV).
28. Fenelon, op. cit., 10.
29. Exodus 33:1 (CEV).
30. Exodus 33:13 (CEV).
31. Harris Collingwood, "Leaders Remember the Moments and People That Shaped Them," *Harvard Business Review Breakthrough Leadership*, 1998, 10.
32. Job 13:15 (KJV).
33. Eldredge, *Wild at Heart*, 105.
34. Fenelon, op. cit., 4.
35. Ibid., 7.

Chapter 5—Practice Consistent Fitness Renewal

1. Jim Rohn, "Jim Rohn Quotes," *BrainyQuote*, https://brainyquote.com/quotes/j/jimrohn147499.html.

2. John F. Kennedy, "John F. Kennedy Quotes," *BrainyQuote*, https://
   www.brainyquote.com/quotes/quotes/j/johnfkenn131489.html.
3. C. J. Prince, "CEOs Anonymous," op. cit.
4. Meryl Davids Landau, "Eight CEO Sacrifices," *Chief Executive*, November 1, 2001.
5. Ibid.
6. Nancie Carmichael, *Praying for Rain* (Nashville: Thomas Nelson, 2001), 4.
7. Fox, *How to Become CEO*, op. cit., Rule V.
8. J. Oswald Sanders, "Lessons I've Learned," *Discipleship Journal* 15: 14.
9. Ibid.
10. Harold J. Chadick, ed., *Best of Fenelon* (Gainesville, FL: Bridge-Logos Publishers, 2002), 58.
11. Presentation to Pastors, American Bible Society, National Church Advisory Council, c. 1998.
12. Leviticus 23:3 (CEV).
13. Eugene H. Peterson, *The Message* (Colorado Springs: NavPress, 2002), 1698.
14. Ibid.; Proverbs 29:25.
15. Daniel 1–2.
16. Psalm 119:96.
17. Carmichael., op. cit., 74.
18. See for example Mark 6:31, 46.
19. Fenelon, op. cit, 69.
20. Ibid., 120.
21. Ibid., 112.
22. Ibid., 87.
23. Sirach 30:15–16 (GNT).
24. 1 Corinthians 3:17; 6:19.
25. Fenelon, op. cit., 111.

26. Ibid., 170.
27. Ibid., 63.

Chapter 6—Cultivate Creativity

1. John Lennon, *Marketing Your Art the Right Way* blog, http://marketingtrw.com/blog/every-child-is-an-artist-until-hes-not-an-artist-John-lennon.

2. Michelangelo, "Michelangelo Quotes," *BrainyQuote*, https://www.brainyquote.com/quotes/quotes/m/michelangelo108740.html.

3. Henri Matisse, "Henri Matisse Quotes," *BrainyQuote*, https://www.brainyquote.com/quotes/quotes/h/henrimatis109310.html.

4. Pablo Picasso, "Quotable Quote," *goodreads.com*, https://www.goodreads.com/quotes/7075-every-child-is-an-artist-the-problem-is-how-to.

5. Eric Metaxas, *Bonhoeffer: Pastor, Martyr, Prophet, Spy* (Nashville: Thomas Nelson, 2010), 51–52.

6. Julia Cameron, *The Artist's Way* (New York: Tarcher/Putnam, 2002), ix.

7. Ibid.

8. Josh Linkner, "8 Ways to Undermine Yourself as a Leader," Forbes, April 26, 2013, https://www.forbes.com/sites/joshlinkner/2013/04/26/8-ways-to-undermine-yourself-as-a-leader/#6cd7b45c7cfa.

9. Joseph Schumpeter, "The Art of Management," *The Economist*, February 11, 2011, 76.

10. Ibid. See also Tom Kelly and David Kelley, "Reclaim Your Creative Self," *Harvard Business Review*, December 2012, 115–118.

11. Chuck Salter, "Every Child Is an Artist," *Fast Company*, September 2013, 82.

12. Ibid.

13. Henry, op. cit., 15.

14. Places like the Center for Creative Leadership (www.ccl.org) can be of help.

15. *English Oxford Living Dictionaries, s.v.,* "charette," https://en.oxforddictionaries.com/definition/us/charrette.

16. See Madeleine L'Engle, *Walking on Water* (Colorado Springs: Waterbrook, 2001), 3.

17. Jeffrey Selingo, *College (Un)Bound* (New York: Houghton Mifflin, 2013).

18. L'Engle, op. cit., 98.

19. Ibid.

20. Ibid., 9–10.

21. *Fast Company,* "Every Child Is an Artist," op. cit.

Chapter 7—Enhance Trust

1. Walter Anderson, "Walter Anderson Quotes," *BrainyQuote,* https://www.brainyquote.com/quotes/quotes/w/walterande183073.html.

2. Lao Tzu, "Lao Tzu Quotes," *BrainyQuote,* https://www.brainyquote.com/quotes/quotes/l/laotzu379183.html.

3. Mona Sutphen, "Mona Sutphen Quotes," *BrainyQuote,* https://www.brainyquote.com/quotes/quotes/m/monasutphe622035.html?src=t_trust.

4. Stephen M.R. Covey, *The Speed of Trust* (New York: Simon and Schuster, 2006), 1.

5. See dictionary.com and webster.com for definitions of "trust."

6. Covey, *The Speed of Trust,* 5.

7. Ibid., 25. See also David DeSteno, "Who Can You Trust?" *Harvard Business Review,* March 2014, 113–115.

8. Habecker, *The Other Side of Leadership,* 41.

9. John W. Gardner, *The Heart of the Matter* (Washington, DC: Independent Sector, 1986), 11. See also Dan Bolin, "Strengthening Leaders," *Outcomes,* Spring 2013, 24–26; Dan Busby, "A

Deficit of Trust," *Focus on Nonprofit Accountability*, Third Quarter 2013, 1–2; and Mark Holbrook, "Humility Is the Key," *Outcomes*, Spring 2013, 38.

10. Covey, op. cit., 1.

11. Gardner, op. cit.

12. Robert C. Pozen, "The Delicate Art of Giving Feedback," *HBR Blog Network*, March 28, 2013, https://hbr.org/2013/03/the-delicate-art-of-giving-fee.

13. See Jack Zenger and Joseph Folkman, *The HBR Blog Network*, March 15, 2013.

14. Manfred F.R. Kets deVries, "Coaching the Toxic Leader," *Harvard Business Review*, April 2014, 100–109.

15. Covey, op. cit., 301.

16. See Habecker, *Rediscovering the Soul of Leadership*, 33–38, for ideas on how to build organizational trust. See also Dan Busby, *Trust* (Winchester, VA: ECPA Press, 2015).

17. Covey, op. cit., 298, 301. See also Adam Bryant, "How to Be a C.E.O., From a Decade's Worth of Them," *The New York Times*, October 27, 2017, https://www.nytimes.com/2017/10/27/business/how-to-be-a-ceo.html.

Chapter 8—Ensure Personal and Organizational Accountability

1. Thomas Paine, "Quotable Quote," *goodreads.com*, https://www.goodreads.com/quotes/287492-a-body-of-men-holding-themselves-accountable-to-nobody-ought.

2. Albert Schweitzer, "Albert Schweitzer Quotes," *BrainyQuote*, https://www.brainyquote.com/quotes/quotes/a/albertschw143119.html.

3. Peter Greer and Chris Horst, *Mission Drift: The Unspoken Crisis Facing Leaders, Charities, and Churches* (Bloomington, MN: Bethany House, 2014).

4. 2 Kings 22:7 (HCSB).

5. 2 Samuel 5:12.

6. Psalm 139:23–24.

7. Habecker, *Rediscovering the Soul of Leadership*, 179–182.

8. Marylou Habecker, "Loneliness and Leadership—the Spouse's View," in Habecker, *The Other Side of Leadership*, 208–215.

9. John O'Neil, *Leadership Aikado: Six Business Practices to Turn Around Your Life* (New York: Harmony Books, 1996), 27.

10. Personal conversations with John Dellenback, former member of Congress from Oregon.

11. Sheila Heen and Douglas Stone, "Finding the Coaching in Criticism," *Harvard Business Review*, January-February 2014, http://hbr.org/2014/01/find-the-coaching-in-criticism/ar/pr.

12. Ibid.

13. Ibid.

14. Zenger and Folkman, op. cit.

15. Heen and Stone, op. cit.

16. Ibid.

17. Ibid.

18. Ibid.

19. Ibid.

20. Ibid.

21. Ibid.

22. Ibid.

23. Habecker, *Rediscovering the Soul of Leadership*, 121–129.

Chapter 9—Embrace the Power of Forgiveness

1. George Herbert, "George Herbert Quotes," *BrainyQuote*, https://www.brainyquote.com/quotes/quotes/g/george-herb397815.html.

2. Walter C. Wright, *Relational Leadership* (Cumbrian, CA:

Paternoster Press, 2000), 201. See also Harriet Hill, Margaret Hill, Richard Bagge, and Pat Miersma, *Healing the Wounds of Trauma* (New York: American Bible Society, 2013), 85–91.

3. Wright, op. cit., 202.
4. Ibid., 203.
5. Habecker, *Rediscovering the Soul of Leadership*, 138–145.
6. Laura Hillenbrand, *Unbroken* (New York: Random House, 2010), 380.
7. Ibid.
8. See oprah.com: "Oprah's Forgiveness Aha! Moment"— "Forgiveness is giving up the hope that the past could have been any different."
9. Van Ryn, Newell, and Cerak, op. cit.
10. Matthew 18:35.
11. 2 Samuel 11–15.
12. 2 Samuel 14:25–33.

Chapter 10—Follow and Lead, Lead and Follow

1. See "Spiritual Dimensions of Leadership," in *ABS Military Bible*, Holy Bible–Good News Translation (New York: American Bible Society, 1992), iii.
2. Aristotle, "Quotable Quote," *goodreads.com*, https://www.goodreads.com/quotes/361140-he-who-cannot-be-a-good=follower-cannot-be-a.
3. Michael Hyatt, "Why the Best Leaders Are Great Followers," michaelhyatt.com, https://michaelhyatt.com/why-the-best-leaders-are-great-followers.
4. Jim Collins, *Good to Great* (New York: Harper Collins, 2001).
5. Ira Chaleff, "Courageous Leaders, Courageous Followers: New Relationships for Learning and Performance," *Ideas for Leaders*, 2001.
6. Gardner, op. cit., 5.

7. See Barbara Kellerman, "What Every Leader Needs to Know about Followers," *Harvard Business Review*, December 2007.

8. Olivia Mellan, "Speaking Truth to Power: How Followers Really Lead," *Investment Advisor*, March 1, 2011.

9. Ibid.

10. Chaleff, op. cit.

11. Gardner, op. cit., 6.

12. 1 Kings 11–12.

13. Chaleff, op. cit.

14. Gardner, op. cit.

15. Ibid.

16. Ibid., 8–9.

17. Ira Chaleff, "New Relationships for Learning and Performance," *Ideas for Leaders*, December 2001.

18. Tom Peters, "Follow the Leader," *Fast Forward*, May 1997.

19. Daniel Katz and Robert L. Kahn, *The Social Psychology of Organizations*, Second Edition (Hoboken, NJ: John Wiley & Sons, 1978), 571.

20. Proverbs 15:31.

21. Mellan, op. cit.

22. Eugene B. Habecker, "Optimizing the Board-President Relationship: Best Practices That Make a Difference!" In *Strategies for University Management, Vol. II*, J. Mark Munoz and Neal King, eds. (New York: Business Expert Press, 2016), 29–40.

23. Heen and Stone, op. cit.

24. Ira Chaleff, "Avoid Fatal Crashes: Leaders and Their Blind Spots," *Leadership Excellence* 29, 10 (October 2012).

25. Richard T. Pascale and Anthony Athos, *The Art of Japanese Management* (New York: Warner Books, 1981), 246.

Chapter 11—Understand That the Greatest Soft Skill Is Love

1. Ramon Llull, *quotefancy.com*, https://quotefancy.com/ quote/1651772/Ramon-Llull-He-who-loves-not-lives-not.

2. Skye Jethani, "Love Is Not a Scarcity," *With God Daily Devotional*, October 18, 2015, https://skyejethani.com/devotional/ love-is-not-a-scarcity.

3. John 15:13.

4. Susan Howatch, *Ultimate Prizes* (New York: Harper Collins, 1996), 6.

5. Peterson, op. cit., 1686.

6. Exodus 15:13a (CEV).

7. 1 Corinthians 13:13 (MSG).

8. Sanders, op. cit., 66.

9. Ibid.

10. Matthew 5:44–46 (CEV).

11. The idea of "understanding backward" has often been attributed to Danish philosopher Soren Kierkegaard.

12. John 17:21–27.

13. "What Kind of Love Is This?" *Word in Life Bible* (Nashville: Thomas Nelson, 1968), 1465.

14. "25 Maya Angelou Quotes to Inspire Your Life," *Goalcast*, https://www.goalcast.com/2017/04/03/ maya-angelou-quotes-to-inspire-your-life.

15. Sanders, op. cit.

16. Based on conversations with Dr. David F. Allen, Director, the Renascence Institute, Nassau, The Bahamas.

17. Peterson, op. cit., 1669.

18. 1 Corinthians 13:4–8 (CEV).

19. Sanders, op. cit.

20. Laurie Kaplan Singh, "Under Scrutiny," *Chief Executive*, November 1, 2001.

Conclusion

1. Wess Stafford, "Finishing Well," *Outcomes*, Spring 2013.
2. Clayton M. Christensen, "How Will You Measure Your Life?" *Harvard Business Review*, July 2010, https://hbr.org/2010/07/how-will-you-measure-your-life.
3. Martin Dewhurst and Paul Willmalt, "Manager and Machine: The New Leadership Equation," *McKinsey Quarterly*, September 2014.
4. Thomas J. Saporito, "Fifty Shades of Gray: The Real World of the CEO," *Chief Executive.Net*, September/October 2015, 22, https://chiefexecutive.net/fifty-shades-of-gray-the-real-world-of-the-ceo.
5. Craig Larson and Brian Lowery, eds., *1001 Quotations That Connect* (Grand Rapids, MI: Zondervan, 2009), 93.

More Praise for *The Softer Side of Leadership*

"When Gene Habecker speaks to the topic of leadership, the wise and prudent person in a position of authority and influence listens. Few people in this world have the depth and breadth of experiences in the position of chief executive as does he. As a veteran of leading noted institutions of higher education, international ministry organizations, and highly regarded faith-based publications, Gene has learned in the arena. In *The Softer Side of Leadership*, he shares lessons that can only come from digging deep into a lifetime of experience and doing so with a servant's heart."

Paul Lowell Haines, EdD, JD, President, Taylor University

"This book is sacred space. If you are a leader seeking to be known as having a soul and a heart full of love for others, this is the place to start. Full of great research and deep personal experience, Gene nails it! He supports his work with biblical balance and several decades of time at the top. His real-life stories bring a sense of realism and practicality. I could not put it down. I suspect I will go back to it again and again. Transform your leadership by taking a look at the softer side."

Nicholas J. Wallace, CPA, Director, BKD, LLP

"Drawing from his wealth of experience as a CEO, his insightful reflections from Scriptures, and his learning from a wide range of literature on leadership, Dr. Habecker has produced a book which is a must read for all who are in leadership roles. His book is full of gems and insights on the soft skills and the much neglected personal, foundational and relational aspects of leadership. I found the perspectives and principles set out in the book also relevant, applicable and helpful to leaders in my contexts in Asia, and I believe, also to leaders in other cultural contexts as well."

Kua Wee Seng, Director,
United Bible Societies China Partnership

"What a good book! I was really challenged by it. It represents a holistic approach to leadership and provides practical ideas on the behaviors, habits, disciplines, and attitudes that leaders must learn and develop that ultimately lead to organizational transformation. Dr. Habecker's style will keep you engaged by providing constructive and relevant examples from more than thirty years as president/CEO. Prepare to be challenged, empowered, and motivated to cultivate the softer side of leadership."

Manuel Rosado, MBA, Vice President/Partner,
Spectrum Investment Advisors, Inc.

"You can trust the teachings of someone who has obtained knowledge both by serious study and by firsthand experience. Gene Habecker has [done] both. With degrees in management and law and a life as a university president, international speaker and consultant, acclaimed author, and beloved husband, dad, and grandfather, he has a track record of providing wisdom, leadership, and vision for anyone who has the privilege to serve with him, certainly myself included."

Dennis E. Hensley, PhD, author,
The Power of Positive Productivity

"This book is a must-read for leaders of any organization. Leaders are often thought to be born as leaders, both ability- and personality-wise, but no one becomes a successful leader without acquiring leading skills. This book on the importance of communication skills for leadership has been written based on the author's many years of experience as a successful leader. The author, my senior colleague, is a person of soft skills. I myself have been blessed by his considerate and patient way of communicating with a non-native English speaker like me. This book teaches us that a leader should always sincerely listen to, share viewpoints with, and trust other people. All leaders should stop to read this book when pressed to focus primarily on the numerical results of their organization."

Makoto Watabe, General Secretary, Japan Bible Society, Tokyo

"Leadership books often invite us to ascend to the top by mastering certain skills. Gene Habecker guides us to descend into the heart to master ourselves. There we find more than a successful career; we find a meaningful life. Following the wise instruction in this book can lead to an experience many leaders miss: joy in one's work."

Rev. Shayne Looper, Lead Pastor, Lockwood Community Church

"Your bookshelves, like mine, may be crowded with leadership books dealing with multiple topics, including the importance of *hard skills*. Interestingly, over years of coaching, mentoring and counseling, I have seldom observed leadership failure from a lack of appropriate application of the hard skills necessary to accomplish job related activities and tasks. Alternatively, I have often seen leadership failures where *soft skills* have been lacking. *The Softer Side of Leadership* identifies and addresses the need for and the importance of *soft skills* in various leadership applications. Personality traits and behavioral competencies are heart and soul issues, occasionally deeply buried, yet transformable as may be required for success in all leadership roles. This book goes beyond *hard skills* and highlights the importance of *soft skills* as a necessary foundation for effective leadership. I heartily recommend it."

Ethan Jackson, former corporate CEO

"In a time when hard skills are no longer enough, Dr. Habecker presents a compelling case for the soft skills needed to be an effective leader. *The Softer Side of Leadership* is a must-read for existing and aspiring leaders alike who seek practical insights into the necessary behaviors, practices, and attitudes of leadership from a decidedly Christian perspective. I was inspired by the content."

**Mary Jo "Jody" Hirschy, PhD, Chair,
Business Department, Taylor University**

"Gene Habecker knows leadership. *The Softer Side of Leadership* is confirmation that knowledge is important, but wisdom and people skills are the ingredients to true leadership success. Without the skills Gene presents, a leader is not fully complete or performing at his or her full potential. It has been my privilege to see Gene not just write about leadership, but to live it out at an extraordinarily high level. Read this book and do what it says, and you will excel in leadership and become the leader God intended you to be."

Roger C. Muselman, MBA Chairman, DRG Holdings, LLC

"With his diverse and extensive experience, Dr. Gene Habecker demonstrates that he has mastered the soft skills of leadership like no one else I know. In this groundbreaking book, Gene shares his personal experiences and insights with refreshing and inspiring vulnerability. These are the qualities that makes him a great transformational, servant leader. I look forward to visiting the pages of this book again and again, implementing Gene's ideas. The material serves as both a catalyst for personal growth and also a rich resource for empowering others to develop essential skills. This book is a must read for leaders who truly value those they serve.

John Guido, MA, President, Verbo Ministries, Cuenca, Ecuador

"Gene Habecker is a both/and leader. He is wired to do the hard skills of leadership well—and this deeply personal book [reveals] how he learned to do the soft skills of leadership effectively. In addition to learning from Habecker's experiences, you will encounter a treasure trove of wisdom from other top-level leaders in the book. *The Softer Side of Leadership* is personal, practical, and probing. It will challenge any leader to keep growing in ways that matter."

Jay Barnes, PhD, President, Bethel University

"Leaders learn best from successful leaders – leaders like Gene Habecker. This book will create regrets of having given too much attention to the *hard skills* of organizational leadership to the neglect of the more life-giving and transformational *soft skills*. This book is at once convicting and motivational. Gene's transparent stories left me with renewed commitment to focus more on those soft skills. Beware, that might happen to you as well!"

Robert C. Andringa, PhD, President Emeritus, Council for Christian Colleges and Universities

"This essential book provides a roadmap for effective leadership. Habecker invites the reader to re-discover the value of the too often *missing* soft skills of leadership. 'Staying connected to the heart does not dominate many lunchroom conversations.' As leaders we are more comfortable exploring the hard realities of our world through charts, tables, analytics, and statistics. Habecker takes the reader through unchartered territory embracing the soft skills within both personal and organizational dimensions. Many aspiring leaders limit their leadership development to gaining more knowledge, competence training, and learning hard skills—what leaders do. 58% of hiring managers in the US said lack of soft skills was limiting their company's productivity. Habecker places emphasis on the value of both hard and soft leadership skills as vital. *The Softer Side of Leadership* challenges the reader to think about *who* we are and *how* we develop leadership with the capability to reflect character, commitment, attitude and emotional health alongside the hard skills. This is the journey Habecker's beautiful book invites the reader to take."

Michael Perreau, Director General, United Bible Societies

"I worked closely with Gene Habecker for the many years that he served as President of Taylor University. In my role as a trustee and as Chairman of the Board of Trustees, I saw Gene in action. His style reflected both the *hard skills* and especially the *soft skills* of leadership. All of us who worked with him respected his ability to use analytical skills in leading a complex organization. But we also saw and appreciated his people skills. In this book he has distilled for our benefit many of the lessons he learned through decades of strong leadership."

Mark Taylor, Chairman/CEO, Tyndale House Publishers

"In his latest book, *The Softer Side of Leadership*, Dr. Habecker emphasizes social concepts like love and honesty as virtues of greater importance for leaders. Such insight bears significance as it is drawn from his years of successful service in leadership positions at university and Christian missionary organizations. Dr. Habecker stresses the importance of these virtues for leaders as he sees that their leadership is not limited to only the organization they belong to. The value and significance of these virtues resonate well in the Asian context, and I strongly recommend this book as a must-read for leaders in Asia."

**Ho Yong Kim, DD, Executive Director,
Korean Bible Society, Seoul**

"Do we *really need another book on leadership?* Read this wake-up call from Eugene Habecker: 'Often, the organization that was being led ten years ago is not the same organization *today that it was then.* The temptation for leaders is to "freeze" what they know about leadership and then move that frozen paradigm into the future.' *Oh, my!* Shoot-from-the-hip leadership with decades-old competencies won't cut it anymore. *You must read this book!*"

John Pearson, author, *Mastering the Management Buckets*

"Too often, universities, businesses, and non-profit organizations focus and reward leadership skills that maximize productivity, innovation, and return-on-investment. While these *hard skills* are critical to the success of any organization, there is growing recognition that the most effective leaders have mastered the *softer side of leadership*. Lacking soft skills such as integrity, character, honest communication, and love for people has resulted in corrupt business practices, cultural clashes, and myopic strategic vision, ultimately destroying leaders and their organizations. Dr. Habecker's research and decades of experience provide candid insights into effective transformative leadership. *The Softer Side of Leadership* is a must-read for everyone to more effectively manage themselves and lead others."

The Honorable Stephen L. Johnson, Administrator of the Environmental Protection Agency (EPA), under President George W. Bush

"A wonderful new collection of thoughts exploring all the critical skills any leader should consider employing. In his latest book, Gene Habecker opens up a lifetime's experience of leadership in business and academia for all to share. He brings rich insights and learning, revealing the full gamut of soft skills needed for effective leadership. He brings this thinking with a careful biblical underpinning to each element. A marvelous and well-considered leadership text for any missiological leader."

Julie Farrar-Tarpey, Consultant, People and Organisational Development, Human Dimensions Development, Ltd, UK

"I had the privilege of being mentored by Dr. Habecker during our work together at the American Bible Society. Gene is definitely a practitioner of the principles he expounds in this book. He is gentle, but firm; affirming, but challenging; trusting but verifying. I recommend this book to anyone who wants to be a transformational leader. It will bring you closer to your goal."

Emilio A. Reyes, DD, Vice President, Latin America, OneHope, Inc.

"Dr. Habecker's new book on leadership presents a fresh perspective on [taken-]for-granted skills required for today's leaders. Charged with decades of personal experiences, coupled with relevant scriptural narratives, and embellished with a [wealth] of literature, this book serves as a daily handbook to equip leaders in their personal development journeys. Organizational principles of creativity, trust, accountability, forgiveness, followership, and love are emphasized with a cultural spin, enabling the readers to relate—personally and professionally—with the benefits of embracing these principles within their organizational culture and setting."

Michael Bassous, PhD, General Secretary, Bible Society of Lebanon

"Gene Habecker presents a vivid picture of not only the key elements of the softer side of leadership but also how they surfaced and were applied in his successful roles as a leader and follower. This is a book that weaves very nicely between theory and practice and is eloquently summed up in Chapter 7 by the words 'authentic, vulnerable, healthy, and filled with grace.' It truly reflects the leader I know and worked with during my nine years at the American Bible Society."

Patrick English, MBA, former Chief Operating Officer and Chief Financial Officer of the American Bible Society

"Gene Habecker is a learner. And that is deeply evident in this book, as well as in his life. The soft skills which he articulates weren't the ones that initiated his career. They were discovered, over time. And they bore fruit. For those who wish to lead for the sake of the Other, *The Softer Side of Leadership* is a must. Enjoy!"

Stan D. Gaede, PhD, President, Christian College Consortium

"*The Softer Side of Leadership* refocuses our attention on the unnoticed motivations of the heart that are often overlooked. Dr. Habecker reminds us that leadership is about people, not just about results and success. I appreciate the transparency he shares through his personal experiences, especially in marriage where the soft skills really come to light. Read this book and you will be reconnected to your own heart, and to God's."

Robert Capaldi, President, Durapower,
an International Import Company, Ecuador

"*The Softer Side of Leadership* is a must read *for everyone*. Whether you identify as a leader or not, you will find practical, life-giving, and essential skills for life. I have read countless books on leadership, yet none frame the topic in the way Habecker does by encouraging the development of the often-overlooked area of soft skills. It is a book you will find yourself coming back to again and again for both vocational and personal purposes."

Kevin Gushiken, PhD, Director, PhD in Leadership,
Capital Seminary and Graduate School

"Dr. Habecker focuses on the heart of the matter in leadership in this book that is relevant in today's global context, especially in India. He draws us to the example Jesus set on the night he was betrayed, when in full knowledge of what was going to happen, Jesus showed the full extent of his love for his disciples by washing his disciples' feet. I fully endorse Dr. Habecker's excellent insight into how leaders develop skills on creativity, mutual trust, accountability, forgiveness, and above all, loving their followers. This book is not just for one time reading but is an important manual for every leader who desires to lead well."

John Amalraj, Leadership Consultant, and former
Executive Secretary, Interserve India

"Eugene Habecker lives out his passion for leading with humility and grace. In *The Softer Side of Leadership*, he brings to life many of the strategies for organizations to adopt to affectively move people to be all that God has created them to be. As someone who has followed Dr. Habecker for many years, I have personally observed his winsome approach to team development, and have been encouraged in my own faith journey of leadership through witnessing his approach to vulnerable and transparent exampleship."

Dr. Sherilyn R. Emberton, President, Huntington University

"The more I study Governance and Leadership in Africa in church and society, the more I get convinced that the question of Leadership is the most important topic to discuss on the continent. Having read two earlier books by Dr. Habecker on Leadership, I wondered whether there was the need for another write up on the same subject. However, as I perused the pages of his latest book, I came to appreciate the *raison d'etre* of *The Softer Side of Leadership*, which I consider a classic piece. The deep penetrating thoughts on modern technology, which was not much of a challenge years ago, have been highlighted in a manner that will challenge present-day-leader thinking. As Dr. Habecker observes, 'The presence of cell phones, iPads and computers, all of which have excellent uses, this hegemony of pervasive personal technology amply dominates and pushes away other good things.' Other pertinent themes raised relate to the need for making time in the busyness of our world.

As one African Head of State has recently stated, 'the challenges that confront Africa which make it poor are not due to the fact that Africa has no resources but that they are due to poor leadership.' This is very true. Having served in both secular and Christian circles I can state emphatically that Africa needs a new kind of leadership, and it is the type of leadership espoused in Dr. Habecker's latest book.

I have known Dr. Habecker and his wife Marylou for more than two decades in both public and private life and I can say with confidence that they walk the talk. Every leader or any person who aspires to leadership will find this book a worthy companion and

I will personally recommend it to colleagues across the continent and beyond."

David Ayi Hammond, Ambassador, African Biblical Leadership Initiative and former Area Secretary for Africa, United Bible Societies

"Dr. Habecker provides a very straightforward guide about how to acquire and cultivate the essential soft skills needed to be transformational in any organization. He reminds us that effective leadership is a combination of hard skills and soft skills. One cannot deny the importance of leaders doing well what they do, things that are measurable and quantitative, such as analytical skills, process development, managing change, projects, and strategic planning and development; nor can one ignore the importance of the professional soft skills that leaders need to have, things that are not necessarily quantitative but qualitative in nature. These soft skills are an integral part of successful leadership. Soft skills focus on how leaders lead and include important aspects such as communication, teamwork, culture, integrity, emotional health, self-management, and focusing intensely on the importance of attitudes and behaviors. Very few books focus on this essential part of leadership. In this book, Habecker covers several important soft skills from both the personal and the organizational dimensions such as the importance of having a sacred space, staying connected to the heart, cultivating creativity, and the power of forgiveness."

Sha' Wilfred, PhD, Professor of Criminal Justice, Valdosta State University, and CEO/Founder, JOST Justice Services and Support

"In his [The] Softer Side of Leadership, noted speaker, author, and university president Dr. Gene Habecker takes readers right into the heart of authentic leadership. For leaders living in an imperfect, broken world, this work is instructional, timely, and inspiring. Dr. Habecker crafts a different kind of leadership, one that avoids the latest trends, focusing instead upon timeless and powerful values that transform the workplace through a lifestyle that exemplifies Christ. This work is recommended reading whether one is in the daily crucible of leadership at work or for the one seeking growth in personal and relational experiences."

Dr. Sandra Gray, PhD, President, Asbury University

Contact Eugene B. Habecker

ebh711@yahoo.com